THE QUOTABLE TOZER II

The Quotable Tozer II

MORE WISE WORDS WITH A PROPHETIC EDGE

Compiled by
Harry Verploegh

Biographical sketch by
Virginia Verploegh Steinmetz

CHRISTIAN PUBLICATIONS
CAMP HILL, PENNSYLVANIA

Christian Publications
3825 Hartzdale Drive
Camp Hill, PA 17011

Faithful, biblical publishing since 1883

ISBN: 0-87509-638-7
LOC Catalog Card Number: 96-84234

Contents

A Biographical Sketch

Aiden Wilson Tozer described himself as an "ignorant seventeen-year-old boy" when he began to listen to preaching on the streets of Akron, Ohio, and responded to Christ's invitation "come unto me all ye that labor." *Find rest, learn my yoke, know lowliness of heart.* Tozer had learned the meaning of labor as the third of six children growing up on the family farm in mountainous Newburg (formerly La Jose), Pennsylvania, near Mahaffey. When Zene, his eldest brother, left the farm around 1907 to work for the Goodrich Rubber Company in Akron, the ten-year-old Aiden did the work of a hired hand and later remarked on his large "ungifted hands," which had done a lot of farm work as a boy.

Although Tozer did not have the advantage of formal education beyond the elementary grades at Wood School, his grandmother taught him what she knew and seemed to have sparked his interest in spiritual realities with her daily habit of consulting a dream book for clues to the significance of objects she had seen in her dreams. On Sundays Tozer read what books were available on the farm. Later when he took a job selling candy, peanuts and books as a "butcher boy" on the

Vicksburg and Pacific Railroad, he recalled that he had not made enough money on the job because he preferred to "sit and read the books from Vicksburg to the end of the line."

After his conversion to Christ, Tozer would withdraw from the constant activity in his Akron home, where his parents took in boarders, to quiet sanctuaries in the attic and basement. There he began his warfare in prayer and an eager search for spiritual realities through the study of Scripture, theology, literature and history, and began to respond to the "fluidity and fullness" of the English language as an instrument for articulating the soul's discovery of God.

The adolescent Tozer's new faith had little nurturing in his own family circle, where no one at that time was a believer, but he joined Grace Methodist Church in Akron and was baptized by immersion in the Church of the Brethren. Determined to obey a call to preach despite his lack of training, he was encouraged in this purpose by Reverend S.M. Gerow, pastor of the Locust Street Christian and Missionary Alliance Church, and became a member of Gerow's congregation. It was at this time that he met Ada Pfautz, whom he married in 1918 when he was twenty-one. It was Ada's saintly mother who, with Gerow, nurtured him in the early years of the Christian life by lending him religious books and acquainting him with her work as a home missionary in the Pentecostal church.

Two years after his marriage, Tozer was ordained as an Alliance minister at Beulah Beach,

Ohio, and he and Ada moved to his first charge in Nutter Fort, West Virginia. On the occasion of his ordination, Tozer wrote a prayer of dedication. In it he accepted the honor of a high and holy calling, but at the same time he took on Christ's yoke of discipline and determined to learn lowliness of heart. Tozer's sense of the sublime and the humble aspects of his call are well expressed in the title he later gave to this prayer when he printed it in *The Alliance Weekly* during his first year as editor. He called his ordination vow "The Prayer of a Minor Prophet."

Lord Jesus, I come to Thee for spiritual preparation. Lay Thy hand upon me. Anoint me with the oil of the New Testament prophet. Forbid that I should become a religious scribe and thus lose my prophetic calling. Save me from the curse that lies dark across the face of the modern clergy, the curse of compromise, of imitation, of professionalism. Save me from the error of judging a church by its size, its popularity or the amount of its yearly offering. Help me to remember that I am a prophet, not a promoter, not a religious manager—but a prophet. Let me never become a slave to crowds. Heal my soul from bondage to things. Let me not waste my days puttering around the house. Lay Thy terror upon me, O God, and drive me to the place of prayer where I may wrestle with principalities and powers and the rulers of the darkness of this world. Deliver me from overeating and late sleeping. Teach me self-discipline that I may be a good soldier of Jesus Christ.

Tozer's dedication as a young pastor to a life of strenuous self-education and courageous resistance to the clerical temptations of compromise, imitations and slick professionalism marked his distinctive ministry of forty-three years—though with characteristic honesty he once said that his spiritual progress had not always been a straightforward but a "zigzag course to heaven." The yoke of Christ, of discipline, which he was called to bear, was not so much the discipline of physical or mental suffering, of pioneer mission work, of persecution, but of spiritual and intellectual preparation for the preaching and teaching ministry. Tozer's yoke was to learn the disciplines of thinking, reading and writing in the service of Christ, of The Christian and Missionary Alliance, and eventually of evangelical Protestants worldwide.

He demonstrated the godly exercise of his gifts in the consistently penetrating quality of his preaching during his pastorates at the Southside Alliance Church in Chicago (1928-1959) and the Avenue Road Church of The Christian and Missionary Alliance in Toronto (1959-1963); in his books of pastoral theology such as *The Pursuit of God* (1948), *The Divine Conquest* (1950) and *The Knowledge of the Holy* (1961); in his biographies of A.B. Simpson (*Wingspread*, 1942) and Robert A.

Jaffray (*Let My People Go*, 1947); in his articles for religious periodicals, his radio talks, his guest preaching series, his high literacy and graphic standards for *The Alliance Witness* and in his influential editorials in that periodical during his tenure as editor from 1950 until his death in 1963.

From the earliest days of his ministry, Tozer was convinced that to be an effective preacher of the Word, he had to develop sensitivity and precision in the use of words. He listened to other preachers and kept a notebook of their clichés. Dead language, powerless to rouse the spiritually dead, was his enemy. After he became editor of *The Alliance Witness*, Tozer issued to those who wrote articles an "index prohibitorum" to protect the periodical from cliché-ridden religious language.

By the time he came to the Chicago church, he realized that he could not use his voice indiscriminately. According to Raymond McAfee, his assistant and choir director during those years, Tozer would place a large volume of Milton's *Paradise Lost* on a music stand and practice modulating his voice by reading the poem aloud. Instead of shouting, he learned to build climactic sentences that would snap and ring, his slight frame rising on tiptoe to match the inflections of his voice.

Tozer kept a spiral notebook in which he copied excerpts from his reading and comments on these passages. The classic English prose writers and poets were his delight. He would regale McAfee or others who provided transportation to meetings with readings from his favorites. His verbal imagination was rich in colorful, sometimes grotesque images and metaphors, which enabled his hearers to see, feel, taste and smell with concrete vividness. In his mouth and in his pen, language was a lively instrument, sometimes exercised playfully in the creative moment, but ever accompanied with the gift of wisdom and spiritual discernment.

Beyond the discipline of his ability to articulate Christian truth, however, was the discipline of those persistent, prophetic emphases by which his ministry is remembered and revered:

—on the worship and knowledge of God,
—on the imperative of unceasing witness to God's grace through worldwide mission,
—on the necessity of courageous criticism of religious practices which would erode the centrality of the person of Christ or make religion a form of entertainment,
—on the power of the Holy Spirit to bring men and women into intimacy with God,
—on the importance of wide reading and the value of absorbing and memorizing Scripture, the classical Christian writers (especially the mystics) and the hymnodists.

Those who heard him preach will recognize the salty eloquence of his reproving voice in this attack on gospel ballad singing:

Gospel ballad singing is now quite the rage in the lower echelon of the entertainment world. Many of the shows beamed toward the paying masses are made acceptable to the religiously inclined by the introduction of a bit of tongue-in-cheek religion, usually expressed in these highly spiced gospel ballads, whose theology is a mixture of paganism and old wives' tales and whose prevailing mood is one of weak self-pity. Such holy men as Elijah, Daniel, Ezekiel and John are turned into burnt-cork minstrels who are made to preach and prophesy for laughs. . . . Every word of Christ, every act, was simple, sincere and dignified. The entire New Testament breathes the same spirit. . . . It is significant that the two greatest movements within the church since Pentecost, the sixteenth century Reformation and the Wesley revival, were characterized by sobriety and sincerity. They both reached the roots of society and touched the masses, yet they never descended to be common or to pander to carnal flesh. The quality of their preaching was lofty, serious and dignified, and their singing the same.

While Tozer might have given more attention to the failure of evangelicals to minister to the lower classes, the marginal peoples of American society, he saw plainly that in their desire to make their gospel respectable and appealing to the rich and powerful, they were creating a Christianity of the bourgeoisie:

> The well-to-do, the upper middle classes, the politically prominent, the celebrities are accepting our religion by the thousands and parking their expensive cars outside our church doors, to the uncontrollable glee of our religious leaders, who seem completely blind to the fact that the vast majority of these new patrons of the Lord of glory have not altered their moral habits in the slightest or given any evidence of true conversion that would have been accepted by the saintly fathers who built the churches.

Despite the wide range of his knowledge of Scripture, theology, history, philosophy and literature, and the recognition given him by individuals and institutions for his intellectual and spiritual stewardship (Wheaton College and Houghton College awarded him honorary doctorates), Tozer was a self-effacing man. When asked to write an article of advice to Christians on books and reading, he began:

> My friends no doubt overestimate my ability to speak wisely on this matter, but in the hope that I may be able to contribute somewhat to the spiritual progress of younger and inexperienced Christians I offer a few words of counsel.

His awareness of the danger of being overestimated by others was an endearing quality about A.W. Tozer. David J. Fant tells us in his study of Tozer's ministry, *A.W. Tozer: A Twentieth Century Prophet*, that when guests came to his parents' home "he would flee out of doors or retreat to the kitchen and if possible eat alone." Lowliness of heart did not have to be learned when his circle of influence was small, but as it increased, he knew his humility would be subject to severe tests.

A member of his Chicago congregation and a friend, Isabel Anderson Chase, remembers how hesitant he was to accept a call to that congregation. He failed to respond at first to the formal invitation of the board and had to be pursued. After Tozer accepted this call, he found it difficult to fulfill the expectations of the congregation as a pastoral visitor to their sick. Though on one particular occasion when he brought communion to a woman desperately ill, Isabel Chase remembers that "the room was hallowed by the presence of the Lord." Tozer found it easy, however, to communicate with babies. He and Ada raised seven children and supported another child through an agency. On one occasion during the Depression after he had visited a needy family in the neighborhood of the Chicago church, he asked members of the congregation to have milk delivered to this home for the children's sake.

Though Tozer's wife assumed the primary responsibility for raising their children, he particularly enjoyed walking to the park with his city-bred youngsters and sharing the lore he knew about trees and birds. Tozer did not follow his children's education closely, but they were expected to do excellent work and develop their God-given talents to the maximum. Because he believed that hothouse Christians tended to be vulnerable and weak, he allowed three of his sons to attend the University of Chicago, where they would develop strength by exposure to many viewpoints. When his children matured, he enjoyed joshing and debating with them. Wendell Tozer recalls that when he lived at home after college, his father would get up early to make his breakfast so they would have maximum bantering time. Occasionally, Wendell reports,

> he would ask my opinion of a book he liked, and if I didn't agree with him that it was a good book, he would say, "When a book and a head come in contact and there is a hollow sound, you can't conclude that the book is empty."

Those who knew him well believe that Tozer's sense of humor was at least one key to his personality. He was a shy and introverted man. His humor was a means of reaching out to others. It was the necessary ballast in the character of a man in pursuit of God.

In his struggle to maintain spiritual integrity, Tozer demonstrated lowliness of heart despite his widening influence in evangelical circles. He was embarrassed if someone did him a special kindness. He was known to accept preaching engagements without remuneration and cared little about money. He once wrote:

> Any of us who have experienced a life and ministry of faith can tell how the Lord has met our needs. My wife and I would probably have starved in those early years of ministry if we couldn't have trusted God completely for food and everything else. Of course, we believe that God can send money to His believing children—but it becomes a pretty cheap thing to get excited about the money and fail to give the glory to Him who is the Giver!

About his possessions he said:

> If I should make out my will, I would have to leave my books to someone. I have a little household furniture, but not too much and not too expensive. With the books, that would be about all.

Having few material possessions, Tozer nevertheless possessed what was most needful for ministry. In his words:

> I was nineteen years old, earnestly in prayer, kneeling in the front room of my mother-in-law's home, when I was baptized with a

mighty infusion of the Holy Ghost. . . . I know with assurance what God did for me and within me and that nothing on the outside held any important meaning. In desperation, and in faith, I took that leap away from everything that was unimportant to that which was most important—to be possessed by the Spirit of the Living God!

Any tiny work that God has ever done through me and through my ministry for Him dates back to that hour when I was filled with the Spirit. That is why I plead for the spiritual life of the Body of Christ and the eternal ministries of the Eternal Spirit through God's children—His instruments.

In one of his sermons as a seasoned prophet, Tozer asked his congregation to pray that he would experience undiminished spiritual power to labor and to bear the yoke of Christ in lowliness of heart to the end:

Pray for me in the light of the pressures of our times. Pray that I will not just come to a wearied end—an exhausted, tired old preacher, interested only in hunting a place to roost. Pray that I will be willing to let my Christian experience and Christian standards cost me something right down to the last gasp!

Virginia Verploegh Steinmetz
Durham, North Carolina

Abandonment to Christ

A man who is always on the cross, just piece after piece, cannot be happy in that process. But when that man takes his place on the cross with Jesus Christ once and for all, and commends his spirit to God, lets go of everything and ceases to defend himself—sure, he has died, but there is a resurrection that follows!R60

~

If Jesus Christ is not controlling all of me, the chances are very good that He is not controlling any of me.Q66

~

The man who surrenders to Christ exchanges a cruel slave driver for a kind and gentle Master whose yoke is easy and whose burden is light.A104

~

I wonder how many Christians in our day have truly and completely abandoned themselves to Jesus Christ as their

1

Lord. We are very busy telling people to "*accept* Christ"—and that seems to be the only word we are using. We arrange a painless acceptance.[T53]

~

We are telling people that the easiest thing in the world is to *accept* Jesus Christ, and I wonder what has happened to our Christian theology, which no longer contains any hint of what it should mean to be completely and utterly abandoned to Jesus Christ, our Lord and Savior.[T53]

~

The devoted and committed person who takes the cross and follows the Lord does not ask what the consequences will be, neither does he argue about God's plan and God's wisdom.[R25]

B

Belief/Unbelief

We can prove our faith by our committal to it, and in no other way. Any belief that does not command the one who holds it is not a real belief; it is a pseudo-belief only. And it might shock some of us profoundly if we were brought suddenly face to face with our beliefs and forced to test them in the fires of practical living.[C49]

~

If you talk about mysticism in our day, every fundamentalist throws his hands high in the air with disgust to let you know that he considers the mystics dreamers, those who believe in the emotion and feeling. But all of those old saints and the fathers of whom I have read taught that you must believe God by a naked, cold intent of your will and then the other things follow along.

A naked intent unto God—those old saints were practical men. They have exhorted us to press on in faith whether we feel like it or not. They have exhorted us to pray—when we feel like it and when we don't. They never taught that we would always be lifted emotionally to the heights. They knew that there are times when your spiritual progress must be by a naked intent unto God.[R51]

3

Those first believers turned to Christ with the full understanding that they were espousing an unpopular cause that could cost them everything. They knew they would henceforth be members of a hated minority group with life and liberty always in jeopardy.D18

~

Moral power has always accompanied definitive beliefs. Great saints have always been dogmatic. We need right now a return to a gentle dogmatism that smiles while it stands stubborn and firm on the Word of God that liveth and abideth forever.G164

~

Unbelief is not just a mental attitude. It is a moral thing. Unbelief is always sinful because it always presupposes an immoral condition of the heart before it can exist.Q45

~

Unbelief is not the failure of the mind to grasp truth. It is not the unsoundness of a logical premise. It is not a bad conclusion drawn from a logical premise. It is a moral sin.Q45

Bible

Even those persons who have never heard of the Bible have still been preached to with sufficient clarity to remove every excuse from their hearts forever. "Which show the work of the law written in their hearts, their conscience also bearing witness, and their thoughts the mean while either accusing or else excusing one another" (Romans 2:15). [A76]

~

The difficulty we modern Christians face is not misunderstanding the Bible, but persuading our untamed hearts to accept its plain instruction. Our problem is to get the consent of our world-loving minds to make Jesus Lord in fact as well as in word. [B114]

~

The great need of the hour among persons spiritually hungry is twofold: First, to know the Scriptures, apart from which no saving truth will be vouchsafed by our Lord; the second, to be enlightened by the Spirit, apart from whom the Scriptures will not be understood. [C37]

~

The saving power of the Word is reserved for those for whom it is intended. The secret of the Lord is with them that fear Him. [G28]

The kind of teaching that I have been giving has disturbed some people. I am not going to apologize at all, because, necessarily, if I have been traveling along thinking I am all right and there comes a man of God and tells me that there is yet much land to be possessed, it will disturb me. That is the preliminary twinge that comes to the soul that wants to know God. Whenever the Word of God hits us, it disturbs us. So don't be disturbed by the disturbance. Remember that it is quite normal. God has to jar us loose.L52

~

Be a Bible meditator.L57

~

Everybody is writing and everybody is talking, but for dying men there is not one word of authority anywhere, except as you hear the sure, true, terrifying words of Jesus Christ.

Literally millions of words are printed every day, but the only authoritative word ever published is that which comes from the Holy Scriptures.O147

~

Read it much, read it often, brood over it, think over it, meditate over it—meditate on the Word of God day and night. When you are awake at night, think of a helpful verse. When you get up in the morning, no matter how you feel, think of a verse and make the Word of God the important element in your day. The Holy Ghost wrote the Word, and if you make much of the Word, He will make much of you. It is through the Word that He reveals Himself. Between those covers is a living Book. God wrote it and it is still vital and effective and alive. God is in this Book, the Holy Ghost is in this Book, and if you want to find Him, go into this Book.P116

~

Falsehoods and deceits are not known in heaven. Never in the blessed kingdom of God has anyone deceived another. The dear old Bible itself is a book of absolute honesty.Q53

~

The sacred page is not to be a substitute for God, although it has been made that by millions of people. The sacred page is not meant to be the end, but only the means toward the end, which is knowing God Himself.R78

~

When the Holy Spirit wrote the epistles, . . . He wrote them and addressed them to certain people and then made them so universally applicable that every Christian who reads them today in any part of the world, in any language or dialect, forgets that they were written to someone else and says, "This was addressed to me. The Holy Spirit had me in mind. This is not antiquated and dated. This is the living Truth for me—now! It is just as though God had just heard of my trouble and is speaking to me to help me and encourage me in the time of my distress!"

Brethren, this is why the Bible stays young always. This is why the Word of the Lord God is as fresh as every new sunrise, as sweet and graciously fresh as the dew on the grass the morning after the clear night—because it is God's Word to man!

This is the wonder of divine inspiration and the wonder of the Book of God![S18]

~

The Bible is the easiest book in the world to understand—one of the easiest for the spiritual mind but one of the hardest for the carnal mind![S147]

~

The one newly converted to Christ is a newborn babe and . . . the Word of God is the milk he needs to make him grow. Keep milk away from the baby a few days, and soon you will have no baby. It must have milk or it will die. So the child of God must depend entirely on the Word of God for his nourishment. [From a sermon]

~

Sermons are good, but they are not to be compared with the Bible as soul food. Songs and hymns are excellent, but let us not become songbook Christians. Men wrote the songs but God wrote the Bible. A successful Christian must be a Bible Christian.[From a sermon]

~

To get a properly balanced diet, we must feed on the *whole Bible*. Certain chapters and verses in the Bible are like pie and cake to our souls, and the temptation is to read them often and to try to live by them alone, neglecting the rest of the Scripture. Jesus said, "Man shall not live by bread alone, but by *every word* that proceedeth out of the mouth of God" (Matthew 4:4, emphasis added).From a sermon

~

Every Christian should read the Bible through chapter after chapter, and book after book, until it is finished: then go back to the beginning and start over again. Only in this way can we get the benefit of "every word" that God has spoken. Let us not skip the "dry" chapters for in them will be found many of the brightest gems of spiritual truths. Let us read the Old Testament as much as the New for it is the foundation upon which the New Testament is built.From a sermon

~

If we are ever to get a deep insight into the holy mysteries of God's Word, we must lay aside every preconceived notion about it and come simply as a child to be taught by the Holy Spirit. God has purposely hidden His truths from the wise and prudent, but He is ready at any time to reveal them unto babes. From a sermon

~

The Holy Spirit wrote the Book, and He is the only One who can impart its truths to the human soul. Let us therefore approach the Scriptures prayerfully, expecting Him to teach us those things which we, left to ourselves, could never discover. He will not disappoint us, for He is come to the world for that very purpose. Jesus said, "The Holy Ghost will teach you all things, and bring to your remembrance whatsoever I have said unto you." From a sermon

~

To get the most out of the Scripture, it must be read slowly and with meditation. David said, "In Thy law do I meditate day and night." In this busy period of the world's history, meditation has become almost a lost art. Everything now is done with a rush. But the child of God will retire to some quiet chamber "far from the maddening crowd," and will find there great enjoyment reading the dear old Book and then quietly ruminating like a true sheep. The world calls time spent in this manner wasted time, but an hour a day invested in such quiet meditation on God's Word will yield dividends in spiritual blessing and bodily health all the rest of our lives. From a sermon

~

God will speak to us if we read and study and obey the Word of God. But when He does speak, we should speak back to Him in prayer and devotion.M41

~

Whenever I find men running to science to find support for the Bible, I know they are rationalists and not true believers!O34

The spirit of the world does not appreciate the Scriptures—
it is the Spirit of God who gives appreciation of the Scriptures. One little flash of the Holy Ghost will give you more
inward, divine illumination on the meaning of the text than
all the commentators that ever commented.[P131]

Body and Soul

Beyond His death and resurrection and ascension, the present work of Jesus Christ is twofold. It is to be an advocate
above—a risen Savior with high priestly office at the throne
of God; and the ministry of preparing a place for His people
in the house of His Father and our Father, as well.

Now it must be said that sin necessitates a separation of
body and soul. While it is proper to say that man is made for
the earth, it is actually necessary to say that man's body is
made for the earth. It was his body that was taken from the
dust of the ground, for man became a living soul when God
breathed into his nostrils the breath of life. The image of
God was not in the body of the man, but in the spirit that
made him man. The body is simply the instrument through
which the soul manifests itself down here—that is all.[T109]

~

God is not ever mad at your body, keep that in mind. The
Lord isn't angry with your body, because your body is just a
poor horse you ride until it crumbles under you and you go
off to heaven.

There is nothing in your body that can do wrong. Your
body is a neutral thing, and it is only your spirit that rules
your body and can lead it wrong.[O133]

It is wrong to place our physical necessities on one side and put praying and singing and giving and Bible reading and testifying on the other side.

How can we say, "This is spiritual" and "This is secular"?

We actually try to walk a tightrope in between . . . the secular and the spiritual, apologizing to God when we must turn aside for a little while to do something "secular." Q138

~

The Lord is the Lord of our bread, the Lord of our eating, the Lord of our bathing, the Lord of our sleeping, the Lord of our dressing, the Lord of our working. When we work we need not say, "Now, Lord, I have to work today, so I'll see You tonight."

Our Lord is with us, sanctifying everything we do—provided it is honest and good. . . . If your job is decent and respectable, the Lord is going to bless it, and if the Lord is in you, He will be in your labor as well.Q138

~

The whole modern notion embodied in our common phrase "soul winning" could stand a good overhauling in the light of the broader teachings of the Scriptures.C 97

~

Every redeemed soul is born out of the same spiritual life as every other redeemed soul and partakes of the divine nature in exactly the same manner.G75

Apart from God Himself, the nearest thing to God is a human soul.[I163]

~

The most godlike thing in the universe is the soul of man.[K3]

~

The soul of man does not change fundamentally, no matter how external conditions may change. The aborigine in his hut, the college professor in his study, the truck driver in the bedlam of city traffic have all the same basic needs: to be rid of their sins, to obtain eternal life and to be brought into communion with God. Civilized noises and activities are surface phenomena, a temporary rash on the epidermis of the human race. To attribute sound values to them and then to try to bring religion into harmony with them is to commit a moral blunder so huge as to stagger the imagination, and one for which we shall surely be paying long after this frenetic extravaganza we call civilization has ended in tragedy and everlasting grief.[N16]

Brotherhood

There is another brotherhood within the brotherhood of humans—it is the brotherhood of the saints of God, for the fact that there is a broad human brotherhood does not mean that all men are saved. They are not. Not until they are saved—born again—do they enter into the brotherhood of the redeemed.[Q29]

13

I believe in the brotherhood of man.

God has made of one blood all people that dwell upon the face of the earth, so that all who are born into the world are born of the same blood. Our skins may be different and our eyes slope in different directions. Some will have red hair and some black, some curly and some straight. We may differ from each other greatly in appearance, but there is nevertheless a vast human brotherhood—all of us descended from that man Adam whose mortal sin brought death and all of its fruits into the world.Q29

~

*T*here is a brotherhood of man which comes by the first birth, and another brotherhood which comes through the second birth. By the grace of God, I want to dwell in that sacred, mystic brotherhood of the ransomed and the redeemed, that fellowship of the saints gathered around the broken body and the shed blood of the Savior!Q30

Change

Nothing that matters is new.[D88]

~

Nothing is new that matters and nothing that matters can be modernized.[D88]

~

Nothing new can save my soul; neither can saving grace be modernized. We must each come as Abel came, by atoning blood and faith demonstrated in repentance. No new way has been discovered. The old way is the true way and there is no new way. The Lamb of God was slain "before the foundation of the world."[D90]

Christ

He can invade the human heart and make room for Himself without expelling anything essentially human. The integrity of the human personality remains unimpaired.[B69]

The message of Christ lays hold upon a man with the intention to alter him, to mold him again after another image and make of him something altogether different from what he had been before.[C 57]

~

Never do the disciples use gimmicks to attract crowds. They count on the power of the Spirit to see them through all the way. They gear their activities to Christ and are content to win or lose along with Him. The notion that they should set up a "programmed" affair and use Jesus as a kind of sponsor never so much as entered their heads. To them Christ was everything. To them He was the object around which all revolved; He was, as He still is, Alpha and Omega, the beginning and the ending.[C 94]

~

When we think of the ebb and flow of man's history and the inability of men to thwart the reality of death and judgment, it seems incredible that proud men and women—both in the church and outside the church—refuse to give heed to the victorious eternal plan and program of Jesus Christ![J 150]

~

Jesus Christ stands alone, unique and supreme, self-validating, and the Holy Ghost declares Him to be God's eternal Son.[P 34]

Jesus Himself had no beauty that we should desire Him. He was not a personality boy. I think He must have been just a plain-looking Jew, for Judas had to kiss Him to tell which one He was. If Jesus had been a television personality and had looked the part, no one would have had to go up and spot Him. They had to spot Him to know who He was among the other Jews.

That's why I think Jesus was a plain-looking man, but when He opened His mouth, glory came out, and men and women either rejected the glory or they followed the glory. But in any case, they knew it was glory, and they knew they could never be the same again.[Q65]

~

Not all of the mystery of the Godhead can be known by man, but just as certainly, all that man can know of God in this life is revealed in Jesus Christ.[R114]

~

Of the many compelling reasons why we ought to know our Savior better than we do, certainly the first is that He is a person, Jesus Christ. We all agree that He is a person, that He is the Eternal Son, but have we gone on to adore Him because He is the source and fountain of everything that you and I are created to enjoy?

He is the fountain of all truth, but He is more—He is truth itself. He is the source and strength of all beauty, but He is more—He is beauty itself. He is the fountain of all wisdom, but He is more—He is wisdom itself. In Him are all the treasures of wisdom and knowledge hidden away!

Jesus Christ our Savior is the fountain of all grace. He is the fountain and source of all life, but He is more than that.

He could say, "I *AM* the life!" He is the fountain of love, but again, He is far more than that—He is love!

He is resurrection and He is immortality and as one of the adoring song writers said, He is the "brightness of the Father's glory, sunshine of the Father's face."[R43]

～

The fact that we are not going on to know Christ in rich intimacy of acquaintance and fellowship is apparent—but why are we not even willing to talk about it? We are not hearing anything about spiritual desire and yearning and the loveliness of our Savior which would break down all barriers if we would move into communion with Him. This appeal is not getting into our books. You don't hear it in radio messages. It is not being preached in our churches.[R43]

～

It is a tragedy if we forget that "earth's fairest beauty and heaven's brightest splendor are all unfolded in Jesus Christ, and all that here shineth quickly declineth before His spotless purity."[R45]

～

Let me remind you of the journey of Jesus Christ to immortal triumph. Remember the garden where He sweat blood. Remember Pilate's hall where they put on Him the purple robe and smote Him. Remember His experience with His closest disciples as they all forsook Him and fled. Remember how they nailed Him to a cross, those six awful hours, the hiding of the Father's face. Remember the darkness and remember the surrender of His spirit in death. This was the path that Jesus took to immortal triumph and everlasting glory, and as He is, so are we in this world![R56]

~

There is excitement in true love, and . . . we Christians who love our Savior ought to be more excited about who He is and what He is![R44]

~

The final key to our lives should be turned over to Jesus Christ.[R58]

~

You cannot trust the man who can only say, "I believe that God revealed Himself through Christ." Find out what he really believes about the person of the incarnate Son of God!

You cannot trust the man who will only say that Christ reflected more of God than other men do. Neither can you trust those who teach that Jesus Christ was the supreme religious genius, having the ability to catch and reflect more of God than any other man.

All of these approaches are insults to the person of Jesus Christ. He was and is and can never cease to be God, and when we find Him and know Him, we are back at the ancient fountain again! Christ is all that the Godhead is![R112]

Some of the teachings in our current Christian circles [say] that Christ is something "added on"—that by ourselves we can have a rather jolly earthly life, but we also need Jesus to save us from hell and to get us into the mansions on the other side!R47

~

How can we be so ignorant and so dull that we try to find our spiritual answers and the abounding life by looking beyond the only One who has promised that He would never change? How can we so readily slight the Christ of God who has limitless authority throughout the universe? How long should it take us to yield completely and without reservation to this One who has been made both Lord and Christ—and yet continues to be the very same Jesus who still loves us with an everlasting love?R133

~

Nothing about our Lord Jesus Christ has changed down to this very hour. His love has not changed. It hasn't cooled off, and it needs no increase because He has already loved us with infinite love and there is no way that infinitude can be increased. His compassionate understanding of us has not changed. His interest in us and His purposes for us have not changed.

He is Jesus Christ, our Lord. He is the very same Jesus. Even though He has been raised from the dead and seated at the right hand of the Majesty in the heavens, and made Head over all things to the Church, His love for us remains unchanged. Even though He has been given all authority and power in heaven and in earth, He is the very same Jesus in every detail. He is the same yesterday, today and forever!

It is hard for us to accept the majestic simplicity of this constant, wonder-working Jesus. We are used to getting things changed so that they are always bigger and better![R134]

~

You and I are not always satisfied with the manner in which God deals with us. We would very much like to do something new, something different, something big and dramatic—but we are called back. For everything we need, we are called back to the simplicity of the faith, to the simplicity of Jesus Christ and His unchanging person.[R135]

~

The very same Jesus—He is the sun that shines upon us, He is the star of our night. He is the giver of our life and the rock of our hope. He is our safety and our future. He is our righteousness, our sanctification, our inheritance. You find that He is all of this in the instant that you move your heart toward Him in faith. This is the journey to Jesus that must be made in the depths of the heart and being. This is a journey where feet do not count.[R135]

~

What a tragedy that in our day we often hear the gospel appeal made on this kind of basis:

"Come to Jesus! You do not have to obey anyone. You do not have to change anything. You do not have to give up anything, alter anything, surrender anything, give back anything—just come to Him and believe in Him as Savior!"[S21]

Contrary to the opinion held by many would-be religious leaders in the world, Christianity was never intended to be an "ethical system" with Jesus Christ at the head.

Our Lord did not come into the world 2,000 years ago to launch Christianity as a new religion or a new system. He came into this world with eternal purpose. He came as the center of all things. Actually, He came to be our religion, if you wish to put it that way.

He came in person, in the flesh, to be God's salvation to the very ends of the earth. He did not come just to delegate power to others to heal or cure or bless. He came to *be* the blessing, for all the blessings and the full glory of God are to be found in His person.[U33]

~

Jesus is in the midst, and because that is true, He is accessible from anywhere in life. This is good news—wonderful, good news![U37]

~

Jesus Christ is the center of the human race. With Him there are no favored races. We had better come to the point of believing that Jesus Christ is the Son of Man. He is not the Son of the first century nor the twentieth century. He is the Son of Man—not a Son of the Jewish race only. He is the Son of all races no matter what the color or tongue.[U39]

~

Christ is at the center of all cultural levels. Preach Christ and show the love of God to the most primitive, most neglected, most illiterate people in the world; be patient and make them understand. Their hearts will awake, the Spirit will illuminate their minds. Those who believe on Jesus will be transformed. This is a beautiful thing that is being demonstrated over and over again in the world today.[U39]

~

Jesus Christ stands in the middle of the human race, at the center of geography, the central figure in time and in the midst of all cultures.[U40]

~

The communion will not have ultimate meaning for us if we do not believe that our Lord Jesus Christ is literally present in the Body of Christ on earth.

There is a distinction here: Christ is literally present with us—but not physically present.

Some people approach the communion table with an awe that is almost fear because they think they are approaching the physical presence of God. It is a mistake to imagine that He is physically present.[U120]

~

When we come to the Lord's table, we do not have to try to bring His presence. He is here![U121]

Our Lord Jesus Christ had no secondary aims. His one passion in life was the fulfillment of His Father's will. Probably He was the only human being after the fall about whom this could be said in perfect terms. With any other person, it can be only an approximation. Realism requires that we say we suppose there never has been anyone who has not mourned the introduction, however brief, of some distraction.

But Jesus never had any distraction or deviation. His Father's will was always before Him, and it was to this one thing that He was devoted.U123

~

Jesus Christ came to help. He came to change our natures. He came to stop old habits of sin. He came to break them and to conquer them.Q102

~

Jesus continually placed His emphasis upon the value and worth of the individual.I168

~

He is the same Jesus—He will always be the same!

He is always the same to the meek, the mourner, the brokenhearted, the penitent sinner. His attitude is always the same toward those who love Him, the honest-hearted person. These are the people who come up to Jesus on the right side—and He never turns them away. He is ready with forgiveness. He is ready with comfort. He is ready with blessing.

We cannot understand this readiness of Jesus to love us and help us and bless us—because He does not really need us. One of His attributes is omnipotence—so He doesn't need us. But the secret is this—He loves us![M144]

~

Everything you need is found in Jesus Christ the Son of God![M145]

~

We make Jesus Christ a convenience. We make Him a Lifeboat to get us to shore, a Guide to find us when we are lost. We reduce Him simply to Big Friend to help us when we are in trouble.[Q20]

~

The Bible knows absolutely nothing about passive reception, for the word *receive* is not passive–it is active. We make the word *receive* into *accept*. Everyone goes around asking, "Will you accept Jesus? Will you accept Him?" This makes a brush salesman out of Jesus Christ, as though He meekly stands waiting to know whether we will patronize Him or not. Although we desperately need what He proffers, we are sovereignly deciding whether we will receive Him or not.[Q32]

~

It is *taking* instead of *accepting*. Whether you are layperson or minister, missionary or student, note this well. Receiving Christ savingly is an act of the total personality. It is an act of the mind and of the will and of the affections. It is thus not only an act of the total personality, it is an *aggressive* act of the total personality.[Q33]

~

To receive Jesus Christ as Lord is not a passive, soft affair—not a predigested kind of religion. It is strong meat! It is such strong meat that God is calling us in this hour to yield everything to Him. Some want to cling to their sinful pleasures. In our churches in this deadly, degenerate, sodomistic hour, we are guilty of making it just as easy as possible for double-minded Christians.[Q35]

Christ's Second Advent

The doctrine of Christ's return has fallen into neglect, on the North American continent at least, and as far as I can detect, today exercises no power whatever over the rank and file of Bible-believing Christians. For this there may be a number of contributing factors; but the chief one is, I believe, the misfortune suffered by prophetic truth between the two world wars when men without tears undertook to instruct us in the writings of the tear-stained prophets. Big crowds and big offerings resulted until events proved the teachers wrong on too many points; then the reaction set in and prophecy lost favor with the masses. This was a neat trick of the devil and it worked too well. We should and must learn that we cannot handle holy things carelessly without suffering serious consequences.[N3]

Who is there that can look more earnestly for the coming of the Lord Jesus than the one who feels that he is a lonely person in the middle of a lonely world?[S17]

Christianity

At the heart of the Christian message is God Himself waiting for His redeemed children to push into conscious awareness of His Presence.[A37]

~

"If any man will," said our Lord, and thus freed every man and placed the Christian life in the realm of voluntary choice.[E38]

~

A man can die of starvation knowing all about bread, and a man can remain spiritually dead while knowing all the historic facts of Christianity.[B68]

~

Christianity is so entangled with the world that millions never guess how radically they have missed the New Testament pattern. Compromise is everywhere. The world is whitewashed just enough to pass inspection by blind men posing as believers, and those same believers are everlastingly seeking to gain acceptance with the world. By mutual concessions men who call themselves Christians manage to get on with men who have for the things of God nothing but quiet contempt.[B111]

~

Orthodox Christianity has fallen to its present low estate from lack of spiritual desire. Among the many who profess the Christian faith, scarcely one in a thousand reveals any passionate thirst for God.[C56]

~

In this quasi-Christian scheme of things God becomes the Aladdin lamp who does the bidding of everyone that will accept His Son and sign a card. The total obligation of the sinner is discharged when he accepts Christ. After that he has but to come with his basket and receive the religious equivalent of everything the world offers and enjoy it to the limit. . . .

This concept of Christianity is in radical error, and because it touches the souls of men it is a dangerous, even deadly, error. At bottom it is little more than weak humanism allied with weak Christianity. . . . Invariably it begins with man and his needs and then looks around for God. True Christianity reveals God as searching for man to deliver him from his ambitions.[D22]

~

Always and always God must be first. The gospel in its scriptural context puts the glory of God first and the salvation of man second. The angels, approaching from above, chanted, "Glory to God in the highest, and on earth peace, good will toward men" (Luke 2:14). This puts the glory of God and the blessing of mankind in their proper order, as do also the opening words of the prayer, "Our Father which art in heaven, Hallowed be thy name" (Luke 11:2, Matthew 6:9). Before any petitions are allowed the name of God must be hallowed. God's glory is and must forever remain the Christian's true point of departure. Anything that begins anywhere else, whatever it is, is certainly not New Testament Christianity.[D22]

~

There is about the Christian faith a quiet dogmatism, a cheerful intolerance. It feels no need to appease its enemies or compromise with its detractors. Christ came from God, out of eternity, to report on the things He had seen and heard and to establish true values for the confused human race.[E129]

~

Evangelical Christians commonly offer Christ to mankind as a nostrum to cure their ills, a way out of their troubles, a quick and easy means to the achievement of personal ends. They use the right words, but their emphasis is awry. The message is so presented as to leave the hearer with the impression that he is being asked to give up much to gain more.[G12]

~

The complacency of Christians is the scandal of Christianity.[G38]

Those Christians who belong to the evangelical wing of the church (which I firmly believe is the only one that even approximates New Testament Christianity) have over the last half-century shown an increasing impatience with things invisible and eternal and have demanded and got a host of things visible and temporal to satisfy their fleshly appetites. Without biblical authority, or any other right under the sun, carnal religious leaders have introduced a host of attractions that serve no purpose except to provide entertainment for the retarded saints.[G135]

~

If we do not make a hard swing back to the very roots of Christian faith and Christian teaching and Christian living, beginning again to seek the face of God and His will, God is going to pass us up![J67]

~

Our trouble is that we are trying to confirm the truth of Christianity by an appeal to external evidence. We are saying, "Well, look at this fellow. He can throw a baseball farther than anybody else and he is a Christian, therefore Christianity must be true. . . ." We write books to show that some scientist believed in Christianity: therefore, Christianity must be true.[L29]

~

In many churches Christianity has been watered down until the solution is so weak that if it were poison it would not hurt anyone, and if it were medicine it would not cure anyone![M31]

We want security in this life and eternal security in the world above! . . . That is a kind of definition of our modern day Christian fundamentalism.M69

~

Christianity is not something you just reach up and grab, as some are taught. There must be a preparation of the mind, a preparation of the life and a preparation of the inner person before we can savingly believe in Jesus Christ.Q17

~

Christianity does vary from itself from place to place and from time to time as it permits itself to be influenced by political, economic, racial or cultural factors. Without doubt neither I who write this nor you who read it can be said to have escaped completely the molding power of society. As Christians we are somewhat different from what we would have been had we lived in a different period of history.N47

~

Where does Christianity destroy itself in a given generation? It destroys itself by not living in the light, by professing a truth it does not obey.O25

~

If you have to be reasoned into Christianity, some wise fellow can reason you out of it! If you come to Christ by a flash of the Holy Ghost so that by intuition you know that you are God's child, you know it by the text but you also know it by the inner light, the inner illumination of the Spirit, and no one can ever reason you out of it.P31

~

Much of our Christianity is social instead of spiritual. We should be a spiritual body with social overtones, but most of our churches are social bodies with spiritual overtones. The heart of the church always ought to be Christ and the Holy Spirit. The heart of the church always ought to be heaven and God and righteousness. They that loved the Lord spoke often one to another, and what they spoke about were spiritual things.P144

~

Evangelical Christianity is gasping for breath. We happen to have entered a period when it is popular to sing about tears and prayers and believing. You can get a religious phrase kicked around almost anywhere—even right in the middle of a worldly program dedicated to the flesh and the devil. Old Mammon, with two silver dollars for eyes, sits at the top of it, lying about the quality of the products, shamelessly praising actors who ought to be put to work laying bricks. In the middle of it, someone trained in a studio to sound religious will say with an unctuous voice, "Now, our hymn for the week!" So they break in, and the band goes twinkle, twankle, twinkle, twankle, and they sing something that the devil must blush to hear. They call that religion, and I will concede that religion it is. It is not Christianity, and it is not the Holy Spirit. It is not New Testament and it is not redemption. It is simply making capital out of religion.Q33

A church can go on holding the creed and the truth for generations and grow old. New people can follow and receive that same code and also grow old.

Then some revivalist comes in and fires his guns and gets everybody stirred, and prayer moves God down on the scene and revival comes to that church. People who thought they were saved get saved. People who had only believed in a code now believe in Christ. And what has really happened? It is simply New Testament Christianity having its place. It is not any deluxe edition of Christianity—it is what Christianity should have been from the beginning.Q18

~

*H*ow can God do His work in people who seem to think that Christianity is just another way of getting things from God?R49

~

*W*hat does the Bible say about true Christianity? It says that if you will take Christ and follow Christ and do what you should about Christ, your Savior, letting Him do what He wants with you, He will certainly take the bitterness out and put His love in. He will take the avarice out and put generosity in. He will take the hatred out and put peace in its place. That is what Christianity teaches and promises.Q102

Christians

*A*t the root of the Christian life lies belief in the invisible. The object of the Christian's faith is unseen reality.A56

If we truly want to follow God we must seek to be other-worldly. This I say knowing well that word has been used with scorn by the sons of this world and applied to the Christian as a badge of reproach. So be it. Every man must choose his world.[A57]

~

Much of our difficulty as seeking Christians stems from our unwillingness to take God as He is and adjust our lives accordingly. We insist upon trying to modify Him and to bring Him nearer to our own image.[A101]

~

Men do not become Christians by associating with church people, nor by religious contact, nor by religious education; they become Christians only by an invasion of their nature by the Spirit of God in the New Birth.[B113]

~

Progress in the Christian life is exactly equal to the growing knowledge we gain of the Triune God in personal experience.[C11]

~

What we need very badly these days is a company of Christians who are prepared to trust God as completely now as they know they must do at the last day. For each of us the time is surely coming when we shall have nothing but God.

Health and wealth and friends and hiding places will all be swept away and we shall have only God. To the man of pseudo-faith that is a terrifying thought, but to real faith it is one of the most comforting thoughts the heart can enter-tain.C50

~

Being has ceased to have much appeal for people and *doing* engages almost everyone's attention. Modern Christians lack symmetry. They know almost nothing about the inner life.C75

~

The body of evangelical believers, under evil influences, has during the last 25 years gone over to the world in complete and abject surrender, avoiding only a few of the grosser sins such as drunkenness and sexual promiscuity.

That this disgraceful betrayal has taken place in broad daylight with full consent of our Bible teachers and evangel-ists is one of the most terrible affairs in the spiritual history of the world.C109

~

It has always been difficult to understand those evangelical Christians who insist upon living in the crisis as if no crisis ex-isted. They say they serve the Lord, but they divide their days so as to leave plenty of time to play and loaf and enjoy the pleasures of the world as well. They are at ease while the world burns; and they can furnish many convincing reasons for their conduct, even quoting Scripture if you press them a bit.D31

The average so-called Bible Christian in our times is but a wretched parody on true sainthood.[E13]

~

Surely this is not the time for pale faces and trembling knees among the sons of the new creation. The darker the night the brighter faith shines and the sooner comes the morning. Look up and lift up your heads; our redemption draweth near.[E133]

~

The cross-carrying Christian, furthermore, is both a confirmed pessimist and an optimist, the like of which is to be found nowhere else on earth.[F13]

~

Let me warn you that if you are a Christian believer and you have found a psychologist who can explain to you exactly what happened to you in the matter of your faith, you have been unfrocked! At the very moment that a man's experience in Christ can be broken down and explained by the psychologists, we have just another church member on our hands—and not a believing Christian![H38]

~

It is only after we yield to Jesus Christ and begin to follow Him that we become concerned about the laxity and thoughtlessness of our daily lives. We begin to grieve about the way we have been living and we become convicted that there should continue to be aimlessness and futility and carelessness in our Christian walk.[H124]

~

In our Christian fellowship, we should be known for being perfectly frank and wholly honest, for honesty has a good root that will also produce other sterling Christian virtues.[I24]

~

God shines in many ways throughout His universe. . . . He shines best of all in the lives of men and women He created and then redeemed.[I166]

~

We have often failed and have not been overcomers because our trying and striving have been in our own strength.[M14]

~

Many solemn, professing Christians will never make any spiritual progress and will never really be happy in the Lord until God finds some way to shake them out of their deadly respectability![R125]

Anyone who brings up the question of consequences in the Christian life is only a mediocre and common Christian.[R25]

~

Christians are obsessed with keeping up that good front.[R58]

~

The praises people try to give us are more dangerous to our Christian walk than their blame.[R139]

~

Many church members start out with a blaze, and then they look around and decide that they should be more like other Christians—just settled down. Soon they are as backslidden as the rest. The amazing thing is that so many people can be so backslidden and never know it![R140]

~

The Christian is not sent to argue or persuade, nor is he sent to prove or demonstrate: He is sent to declare, "Thus saith the Lord." When he has done this he makes God responsible for the outcome. No one knows enough and no one *can* know enough to go beyond this. God made us for Himself: That is the first and last thing that can be said about human existence and whatever more we add is but commentary.[N38]

All of the Christians I meet who are amounting to anything for God are Christians who are very much out of key with their age—very, very much out of tune with their generation.[O151]

~

Most modern Christians live sub-Christian lives![R12]

~

A Christian ought always to be a Christian. . . . He is no Christian if he has to wait for an atmosphere to practice his religion. . . . A Christian is no Christian if he has to go to church to be blessed. A Christian is no Christian until he is all Christian, until he has reached the point of no return. Not seasonal, anymore—but regular at all times. Then the Lord says, he is a disciple indeed.[Q68]

~

If it were true that the Lord would put the Christian on the shelf every time he failed and blundered and did something wrong, I would have been a piece of statuary by this time! I know God and He isn't that kind of God. He will bring judgment when judgment is necessary, but the Scriptures say that judgment is God's strange work. Where there is a lifetime of rebellion, hardened unbelief, love of sin and flagrant refusal of His love and grace, judgment will fall. But with His dear children, God watches over us for spiritual growth and maturity, trying to teach us how necessary it is for us to trust in Him completely and to come to a complete distrust of ourselves.[R101]

It is amazing that genuine Christians are not willing to stand up wherever they are and give a good word for the Lord. There are great political ideologies sweeping the world now whose members will make double-eyed, long-eared donkeys of themselves for the sake of the party and the cause. There are religious sects whose witnesses are willing to go to jail, to be pushed around, to be lampooned for the sake of a miserable, twisted doctrine! But in our Christian ranks, we prefer to be respectable and smooth, and we have a reputation for being very solemn Christian believers.[R125]

~

It is easily possible for a Christian believer to be the loneliest person in the world under a set of certain circumstances. This sense of not belonging is a part of our Christian heritage. That sense of belonging in another world and not belonging to this one steals into the Christian bosom and marks him off as being different from the people around him. Many of our hymns have been born out of that very loneliness, that sense of another and higher citizenship![S17]

Today, as in all the centuries, true Christians are an enigma to the world, a thorn in the flesh of Adam, a puzzle to angels, the delight of God and a habitation of the Holy Spirit.[S143]

~

There are so many things that are done in the world by Christians that are not really bad—they are just trivial.[U125]

~

Today, professing Christians are on the defensive, trying to prove things that a previous generation never doubted. We have allowed unbelievers to get us in a corner and have given them the advantage by permitting them to choose the time and place of encounter.

We smart under the attack of the quasi-Christian unbeliever, and the nervous, self-conscious defense we make is called "the religious dialogue."

Under the scornful attack of the religious critic, real Christians, who ought to know better, are now "rethinking" their faith.U154

~

Christian believers have been going through a process of indoctrination and brainwashing, so it has become easy for us to adopt a kind of creed that makes God to be our servant instead of our being God's servant.M25

~

There are a thousand ways in which we try to use the Lord. What about that young fellow studying for the ministry studying until his eyesight begins to fail, but he wants to use Jesus Christ to make him a famous preacher. They will ordain him, and he will get the title of Reverend and if he writes a book, they will make him a Doctor. But if he has been using Jesus Christ, he is just a common huckster buying and selling and getting gain, and the Lord would drive him out of the temple along with the rest.M73

~

Christian testimony has created a certain expectation in the minds of our friends, and rather than jeopardize our standing with them we dutifully act in accordance with their expectations even though we have no personal conviction about the matter. We are simply afraid not to do what people expect of us. We cannot face our public after we have failed to do what we know they expected us to do.[E98]

~

People testify about their search for the deeper Christian life and it sounds as though they would like to be able to get it in pill form.[M73]

~

"Once it was the blessing, now it is the Lord. Once His gift I wanted, now Himself alone."

This is the basic teaching of the deeper Christian life. It is the willingness to let Jesus Christ Himself be glorified in us and through us. It is the willingness to quit trying to use the Lord for our ends and to let Him work in us for His glory.

That is the kind of revival I am interested in and the only kind—the kind of spiritual reviving and renewing that will cause people to tremble with rapture in the presence of the Lord Jesus Christ.[M77]

Church

To the absence of the Spirit may be traced that vague sense of unreality which almost everywhere invests religion in our times. In the average church service the most real thing is the shadowy unreality of everything. The worshiper sits in a state of suspended mentation; a kind of dreamy numbness creeps upon him; he hears words but they do not register; he cannot relate them to anything on his own life-level. He is conscious of having entered a kind of half-world; his mind surrenders itself to a more or less pleasant mood which passes with the benediction, leaving no trace behind. It does not affect anything in his everyday life. He is aware of no power, no Presence, no spiritual reality. There is simply nothing in his experience corresponding to the things which he heard from the pulpit or sang in the hymns.[B90]

~

Most of us are acquainted with churches that teach the Bible to their children from their tenderest years, give them long instruction in the catechism, drill them further in pastors' classes and still never produce in them a living Christianity nor a virile godliness. Their members show no evidence of having passed from death unto life.[C 35]

~

It seems to me a significant, if not a positively ominous, thing that the words "program" and "programming" occur so frequently in the language of the church these days.[C 92]

~

The average service in gospel circles these days is kept alive by noise. By making a lot of religious din we assure our faltering hearts that everything is well and, conversely, we suspect silence and regard it as a proof that the meeting is "dead." Even the most devout seem to think they must storm heaven with loud outcries and mighty bellowings or their prayers are of no avail.[C 145]

~

The stodgy pedestrian mind does no credit to Christianity. Let it dominate the church long enough and it will force her to take one of two directions: either toward liberalism, where she will find relief in a false freedom, or toward the world, where she will find an enjoyable but fatal pleasure.[D95]

~

Were some watcher or holy one from the bright world above to come among us for a time with the power to diagnose the spiritual ills of church people there is one entry which I am quite sure would appear on the vast majority of his reports: *Definite evidence of chronic spiritual lassitude; level of moral enthusiasm extremely low.*[E7]

~

The dead church holds to the shell of truth without surrendering the will to it, while the church that wills to do God's will is immediately blessed with a visitation of spiritual powers.[F93]

~

One of the greatest weaknesses in the modern church is the willingness to lay down foundations of truth without ever backing them up with moral application![S120]

The church is found wherever the Holy Spirit has drawn together a few persons who trust Christ for their salvation, worship God in spirit and have no dealings with the world and the flesh. The members may by necessity be scattered over the surface of the earth and separated by distance and circumstances, but in every true member of the church is the homing instinct and the longing of the sheep for the fold and the Shepherd. Give a few real Christians half a chance and they will get together and organize and plan regular meetings for prayer and worship. In these meetings they will hear the Scriptures expounded, break bread together in one form or another according to their light, and try as far as possible to spread the saving gospel to the lost world.

Such groups are cells in the Body of Christ, and each one is a true church, a real part of the greater church. It is in and through these cells that the Spirit does His work on earth. Whoever scorns the local church scorns the Body of Christ.[N25]

~

For the very reason that the church is one body, anything that tends to introduce division is an evil, however harmless, or even useful, it may appear to be. Yet the average evangelical church is divided into fragments which live and work separate from, and sometimes in opposition to, each other. In some churches there is simply no time or place for the worship and service of all members unitedly. These churches are organized to make such unity impossible.[N55]

~

In our local assemblies we are part of the church founded by the Lord Jesus Christ and perpetuated by the mystery of the new birth. Therefore our assembly is that of Christian believers gathered unto a Name to worship and adore that Presence.

If this is true—and everything within me witnesses that it is—all the strain is gone. I mean the strain is gone even about traditional religious forms—the pressures that we must sing certain songs, recite certain prayers and creeds, follow accepted patterns in ministerial leadership and service. All of these begin to pale in importance as we function in faith as the people of God who glorify the Name that is above every name and honor His Presence![U27]

~

When you are trying to find out the condition of a church, do not just inquire whether it is evangelical. Ask whether it is an evangelical rationalistic church that says, "The text is enough," or whether it is a church that believes that the text plus the Holy Spirit is enough.[Q20]

~

It is not the form that makes the church or its service. The Presence and the Name—these make the church.[U24]

~

If there is any place in the whole world where we ought to be honest, it is in the church of God.[Q54]

*L*arge or small—it must be an assembly of believers brought together through a Name to worship a Presence. The blessed thing is that God does not ask whether it is a big church or a little church.[U24]

~

*T*he Christian church cannot rise to its true stature in accomplishing the purposes of God when its members operate largely through the gifts of nature, neglecting the true gifts and graces of the Spirit of God.

Much of the religious activity we see in the churches is not the eternal working of the Eternal Spirit, but the mortal working of man's mortal mind—and that is raw tragedy![U93]

~

*R*eligious "activists" have many things of which they can boast. They build churches. They write hymns and books. Musically, they sing and play. Some of them will take time to engage in prayer. Others will organize movements and crusades and campaigns.

No matter how early in the morning they begin and no matter how late at night they stay with their project, if it is an exercise in human talent for religious purposes, it can only wind up as a mortal brain doing a mortal job.

And across it God will write a superscription: "It came to die and it came to go!"

I have taken the pains to say all of this as a reminder that mortality and temporality are written all across the Church of Christ in the world today because so many persons are trying to do with human genius and power of the flesh what only God can do through the Holy Spirit.[U99]

There's an awesomeness about God which is missing in our day altogether; there's little sense of admiring awe in the Church of Christ these days.[K5]

Conduct

Sometimes you are going farther when you are not going anywhere; you are moving faster when you are not moving at all; you are learning more when you think you have stopped learning.[L25]

~

You are just doing what you are—and what you are doing *proves* what you are![Q95]

~

I cannot think of even one lonely passage in the New Testament which speaks of Christ's revelation, manifestation, appearing or coming that is not directly linked with moral conduct, faith and spiritual holiness.[S145]

Conscience

God has given us a faithful witness inside of our own being. . . . It is able to single a man out and reveal his loneliness, the loneliness of a single soul in the universe going on to meet an angry God. That's the terror of the conscience.[Q75]

Conscience never deals with theories. Conscience always deals with right and wrong and the relation of the individual to that which is right or wrong.Q77

~

That Light that has come into the world, which lights every man that comes into the world, is the ground of moral conscience. However it operates, that is its ground. That is why it is here. Because the living, eternal Word is present in the world, present in human society, secretly present, humanity has a secret awareness of moral values.Q78

~

Conscience singles you out as though nobody else existed.Q77 The lonely soul—lonely in the universe with only that soul and an angry God—that's the terror of conscience. And that's exactly what the conscience does—it singles a man out!O103

~

The devil has used bubble-headed, dreamy-eyed boys with pseudo-learning, who know just enough to be pitifully ignorant, and they have laughed conscience out of court.O103

~

That power of conscience that God has set in the human breast suddenly can isolate a soul and hang it between heaven and hell, as lonely as if God had never created but one soul—that's not a joking matter. . . .

Be sure you don't laugh at something that God takes seriously. Conscience is one of those things!O106

~

Remember the conscience is always on God's side—always on God's side! It judges conduct in the light of the moral law, and as the Scripture says, excuses or accuses.O106

Creation/Creator

If we miss seeing God in His works we deprive ourselves of the sight of a royal display of wisdom and power so elevating, so ennobling, so awe-inspiring as to make all attempts at description futile. Such a sight the angels behold day and night forever and ask nothing more to make them perpetually satisfied.E120

~

The heavens and the earth were intended to be a semitransparent veil through which moral intelligences might see the glory of God (Psalm 19:1-6; Romans 1:19-20), but for sin-blinded men this veil has become opaque. They see the creation but do not see through it to the Creator; or what glimpses they do have are dim and out of focus. It is possible to spend a lifetime admiring God's handiwork without acknowledging the presence of the God whose handiwork it is.E114

If God had made all the stars in heaven according to a uniform pattern of size and distance from the earth, it would be like gazing at a glaring theater marquee rather than at the mysterious, wonderful heaven of God that we see when the skies are clear. J109

~

I believe that He created man out of no external necessity. I believe it was an internal necessity. God, being the God He was and is, and being infinitely perfect and infinitely beautiful and infinitely glorious and infinitely admirable and infinitely loving, out of His own inward necessity had to have some creature that was capable of admiring Him and loving Him and knowing Him. So God made man in His own image; in the image and likeness of God made He him; and He made him as near to being like Himself as it was possible for the creature to be like the Creator. K3

The Cross

The devoted and committed person who takes the cross and follows the Lord does not ask what the consequences will be, neither does he argue about God's plan and God's wisdom. R25

~

The world crucified Jesus because they couldn't stand Him! There was something in Him that rebuked them and they hated Him for it and finally crucified Him. L44

Was there ever a cross that was convenient? Was there ever a convenient way to die? I have never heard of any, and judgment is not going to be a matter of convenience, either!M48

～

One of the reasons we exhibit very little spiritual power is because we are unwilling to accept and experience the fellowship of the Savior's sufferings, which means acceptance of His cross.M91

～

Oneness with Christ means to be identified with Christ, identified with Him in crucifixion. But we must go on to be identified with Him in resurrection as well, for beyond the cross is resurrection and the manifestation of His Presence.M93

～

The children of God must be ready for everything the cross brings or we will surely fail the test! It is God's desire to so deal with us about all of the things that the world admires and praises that we will see them in their true light. He will treat us without pity because He desires to raise us without measure—just as He did with His own Son on the cross!M95

～

It is the love and the pity of God for His children that prescribes the chastening of a cross so that we may become the kind of mature believers and disciples that He wants us to be.M97

~

God will crucify without pity those whom He desires to raise without measure!M96

~

The cross of Christ is revolutionary, and if we are not ready to let it be revolutionary in us nor let it cost us anything or control us in any way, we are not going to like a church that takes the things of God seriously.

People want the benefits of the cross but yet they do not want to bow to the control of the cross. They want to take all the cross can offer but they don't want to be under the Lordship of Jesus.P17

~

If the cross of Jesus Christ means what it should to us and we know that we must carry it and die on it and then rise and live above it, we will have a constant desire to advance and gain spiritual ground!R10

~

We talk a lot about the deeper life and spiritual victory and becoming dead to ourselves—but we stay very busy rescuing ourselves from the cross. That part of ourselves that we rescue from the cross may be a very little part of us, but it is likely to be the seat of our spiritual troubles and our defeats.[R59]

~

The cross that we want is that which will come to us from being in the will of God. It is not a cross on a hill nor a cross on a church. It is not the cross that can be worn around the neck. It must be the cross of obedience to the will of God, and we must embrace it, each believer for himself![R73]

~

What a pathetic thing to see the cross so misunderstood in sections of Christianity. Think of poor souls who have never found the evangelical meaning and assurance of atonement and justification, cleansing and pardon. When they come to the time of death, the best they know is to clutch some manufactured cross to the breast, holding it tightly and hoping for some power to come from painted metal or carved wood to take them safely over the river.[R73]

Devil/Satan

Human nature tends to excesses by a kind of evil magnetic attraction. We instinctively run to one of two extremes, and that is why we are so often in error.

A proof of this propensity to extremes is seen in the attitude of the average Christian toward the devil. I have observed among spiritual persons a tendency either to ignore him altogether or to make too much of him. Both are wrong.D40

~

The best way to keep the enemy out is to keep Christ in. The sheep need not be terrified by the wolf; they have but to stay close to the shepherd. It is not the praying sheep Satan fears but the presence of the Shepherd.D43

~

It is ironic that the devil gives the world all of its extremists in every realm—entertainment, politics, society, education, anarchy, intrigue—you name it! Yet it is the same devil that frightens believers about the great danger of becoming "extreme."M11

There are references in the Bible to the devil's wiles and his shrewdness. But when he gambled on his ability to unseat the Almighty he was guilty of an act of judgment so bad as to be imbecilic.[O112]

Disciples

True discipleship is obeying Jesus Christ and learning of Him and following Him and doing what He tells you to do, keeping His commandments and carrying out His will. That kind of a person is a Christian—and no other kind is.[Q20]

~

A true disciple has not taken an impulsive leap in the dark. That person is one who has become a Christian after deep thought and proper consideration.[Q63]

~

A true disciple has reached the point in Christian experience where there is no turning back. Follow him or her for 24 hours of the day and night. You will find you can count on that person's faithfulness to Christ and his or her joyful abiding in the Word of God.[Q63]

~

A true disciple has felt the sense of personal sin and the need to be released from it.[Q63]

There is nothing that Jesus has ever done for any of His disciples that He will not do for any other of His disciples![M143]

~

A true disciple has allowed the Word of God to search his or her heart.[Q63]

~

A true disciple has come to believe that Jesus Christ is the only person who can release him or her from guilt.[Q63]

~

A true disciple has committed himself or herself without equivocation, without reservation to Jesus Christ the Savior.[Q63]

~

A true disciple does not consider Christianity a part-time commitment. That person has become a Christian in all departments of his or her life. [Q63]

~

Christianity on impulse is not the answer to discipleship. God isn't going to stampede us into the kingdom of God.[Q64]

As Christian disciples, we should be whatever we are wherever we are. Like a diamond. A diamond doesn't adjust—it is always a diamond.

And so, Christians ought always to be Christians. We are not Christians if we have to wait for the right atmosphere to practice our religion. We are not Christians if we have to go to church to be blessed. We are not Christians until we are thoroughly Christ's—until we have reached the point of no return, not seasonal anymore—but regular always. Then, the Lord says, we are real disciples. We are following on to know the Lord![Q68]

Doctrine

A doctrine has practical value only as far as it is *prominent in our thoughts* and *makes a difference in our lives.*[B65]

~

Theological truth is useless until it is obeyed. The purpose behind all doctrine is to secure moral action.[E27]

~

Many of the doctrinal divisions among the churches are the result of a blind and stubborn insistence that truth has but one wing.[F59]

Doctrine

In matters of spiritual blessing and victory, we are not dealing with doctrines—we are dealing with the Lord of all doctrine! We are dealing with a Person who is the Resurrection and the Life and the Source from whom flows all doctrine and all truth.[R133]

E

Education

We are turning out from the Bible schools of this country year after year young men and women who know the theory of the Spirit-filled life but do not enjoy the experience. These go out into the churches to create in turn a generation of Christians who have never felt the power of the Spirit and who know nothing personally about the inner fire.[C 88]

~

What we need is not more instruction; we've been instructed to death. Where in the world is there more fundamental Bible teaching than here in Chicago? This is the Mecca of Fundamentalism. This is the Vatican of Evangelicalism.[G105]

~

Perception of ideas rather than the storing of them should be the aim of education. The mind should be an eye to see with rather than a bin to store facts in. The man who has been taught by the Holy Spirit will be a seer rather than a scholar. The difference is that the scholar sees and the seer sees through; and that is a mighty difference indeed.[G150]

*I*t takes more than education to change a man's human nature. Education may bring about certain restraints and some degree of control, but just let a man act freely from within, and you will find out what he really is.Q96

~

*W*e use education and our laws to damp the fires down a little bit, but the old ancient fires of Adam are still there in nature.Q98

~

*S*ome people say they are helped in their faith through the offerings of science and the answers of education. I have a little book in my study (I use it for a window prop when I want to get more air) that has chapters entitled, "Finding God through Science," "Finding God through Nature," "Finding God through Art." Why should we be trying to find God through a back door? Why should we always be peering out of some cellar window looking for God when the whole top side of the building is made of sheer crystal and God is shining down—revealed? We need to open the skylights of our hearts, look up and invite God in.Q159

Entertainment

*W*e now demand glamour and fast-flowing dramatic action. A generation of Christians reared among push buttons and automatic machines is impatient of slower and less direct methods of reaching their goals. We have been trying to apply machine-age methods to our relations with God. We read our chapter, have our short devotions and rush away, hoping to make up for our deep inward bankruptcy by attending another gospel meeting or listening to another thrilling story told by a religious adventurer lately returned from afar.

The tragic results of this spirit are all about us: shallow lives, hollow religious philosophies, the preponderance of the element of fun in gospel meetings, the glorification of men, trust in religious externalities, quasi-religious fellowships, salesmanship methods, the mistaking of dynamic personality for the power of the Spirit. These and such as these are the symptoms of an evil disease, a deep and serious malady of the soul.[A69]

~

We have been forced to look elsewhere for our delights and we have found them in the dubious artistry of converted opera singers or the tinkling melodies of odd and curious musical arrangements. We have tried to secure spiritual pleasures by working upon fleshly emotions and whipping up synthetic feeling by means wholly carnal.[B81]

~

The things you read will fashion you by slowly conditioning your mind. . . .

The same thing is certainly true of the power of modern films on the minds and morals of those who give themselves over to their influences.[J141]

*T*oday more than ever we Christians need to learn how to sanctify the ordinary. This is a blasé generation. People have been overstimulated to the place where their nerves are jaded and their tastes corrupted. Natural things have been rejected to make room for things artificial. The sacred has been secularized, the holy vulgarized and worship converted into a form of entertainment.[D68]

~

*I*n this day when shimmering personalities carry on the Lord's work after the methods of the entertainment world, it is refreshing to associate for a moment, even in the pages of a book, with a sincere and humble man who keeps his own personality out of sight and places the emphasis upon the in-working of God.[E17]

~

*W*ith Bibles under their arms and bundles of tracts in their pockets, religious persons now meet to carry on "services" so carnal, so pagan, that they can hardly be distinguished from the old vaudeville shows of earlier days. And for a preacher or a writer to challenge this heresy is to invite ridicule and abuse from every quarter.[E18]

~

*I*t is now common practice in most evangelical churches to offer the people, especially the young people, a maximum of entertainment and a minimum of serious instruction. It is scarcely possible in most places to get anyone to attend a meeting where the only attraction is God. One can only conclude that God's professed children are bored with Him for they must be wooed to meeting with a stick of striped candy in the form of religious movies, games and refreshments.G136

~

Many are settling for far less than God is waiting to give. They try to stay happy by adding something to their religion that tickles their carnality from the outside. They introduce converted cowboys and half-converted movie actors, and I think they would even stoop to talking horses and gospel dogs to be able to join in saying, "We had a wonderful time!" They will pay a big price to feature some "90-day wonder" so they can get the people to crowd in.M44

~

In our day we must be dramatic about everything. We don't want God to work unless He can make a theatrical production of it. We want Him to come dressed in costumes with a beard and with a staff. We want Him to play a part according to our ideas. Some of us even demand that He provide a colorful setting and fireworks as well!M72

~

A great company of evangelicals has already gone over into the area of religious entertainment so that many gospel churches are tramping on the doorstep of the theater.M112

One of the most popular current errors . . . is the notion that as times change the church must change with them. Christians must adapt their methods by the demands of the people. If they want ten-minute sermons, give them 10-minute sermons. If they want truth in capsule form, give it to them. If they want pictures, give them plenty of pictures. If they like stories, tell them stories. If they prefer to absorb their religious instruction through the drama, go along with them—give them what they want. "The message is the same, only the method changes," say the advocates of compromise.[N15]

F

Faith/Reason

The position of some would-be teachers, which insists that
when you come into the kingdom of God by faith you immediately have all there is in the kingdom of God, is as deadly as
cyanide. It kills all hope of spiritual advance and causes many
to adopt what I call "the creed of contentment."[M52]

~

Faith in God is all but gone. When the Son of Man cometh,
will He find faith on the earth?

Don't you be taken in by statistics—those that say there is
a resurgence of religion, that more people are buying books
about religion and more people going to church. Faith in
God actually is becoming a rarity![O119]

~

Peace of heart does not come from denying that there is
trouble, but comes from rolling your trouble on God. By
faith you have the right to call on One who is your brother,
the Son of Man who was also the Son of God. And if He's
going to look after you, why should you worry at all![O131]

People have faith in "faith"—and largely forget that our confidence is not in the power of faith but in the Person and work of the Savior, Jesus Christ.Q41

~

We have full confidence in Jesus Christ. He is the origin, source, foundation and resting place for all of our faith. In that kingdom of faith, we are dealing with Him, with God Almighty, the One whose essential nature is holiness, the One who cannot lie.

Our confidence rises as the character of God becomes greater and more trustworthy to our spiritual comprehension. The One with whom we deal is the One who embodies faithfulness and truth—the One who cannot lie.Q41

~

I am not insisting that human reason and faith in God are contrary to one another, but I do insist that one is above the other. When we are true believers in God's truth, we enter another world—a realm that is infinitely above reason.Q42

~

Faith never goes contrary to reason—faith simply ignores reason and rises above it.Q42

~

Reason cannot prove that Jesus took upon Himself the form

of a man and that He died for the sins of the world, but faith knows that He did.Q46

~

Reason cannot prove that on the third day Jesus rose from the dead, but faith knows that it happened, for faith is an organ of knowledge.Q46

~

Reason cannot say, "I know that Jesus will come to judge the living and the dead," but faith knows that He will come.Q47

~

Reason cannot say, "My sins are gone," but faith knows that they are forgiven and forgotten.Q47

~

Faith simply ignores reason and rises above it. The brain just comes struggling along behind like a little boy trying to keep up with his dad.Q47

~

The genuine child of God is someone who cannot be explained by human reasoning.Q47

*F*aith is the highest kind of reason after all, for faith goes straight into the presence of God.Q47

~

*W*e may not be astronomers, but we can know the God who made the stars. We may not be physicists, but we can know the God who made mathematics. There may be many technical and local bits of knowledge that we do not have, but we can know the God of all knowledge. We can enter beyond the veil into His very presence. There we stand hushed and wide-eyed as we gaze and gaze upon the wonders of Deity.

It is faith that takes us there, and reason cannot disprove anything that faith discovers and knows. Reason can never do that.Q48

~

*F*aith in God—not in any god, not in religion—but faith in the sovereign God who made heaven and earth, who judges among the gods, whose throne is justice and judgment and who will require men's deeds—that's the God we must believe in, my friends.

And when we believe in that kind of God, we will change our way of living, and we'll change for the better. We will repent, and we will reform and turn to God, and we will cease to do evil and begin to do good, and turn from the world.

We will seek to crucify our flesh and put on the new man which is renewed in holiness.O118

Whatever men may think of human reason God takes a low view of it.[B78]

~

Everything was created for a purpose and I claim that there are some things that human reason cannot do, things that are beyond its capacity.

Reason cannot tell us that Jesus Christ should be born of a virgin, but faith knows that He was.

Reason cannot prove that Jesus took upon Him the form of a man and that He died for the sins of the world, but faith knows that He did.

Reason cannot prove that on the third day Jesus arose from the dead, but faith knows that He did, for faith is an organ of knowledge.

The rationalists take the position that the human brain alone is the organ of knowledge, but they either forget or overlook completely that feeling is a means of knowledge, and so is faith.[Q46]

~

In this relationship with Jesus Christ through the new birth, something takes place by the ministry of the Spirit of God which psychology cannot explain. This is why I must contend that faith is the highest kind of reason after all, for faith goes straight into the presence of God. Our Lord Jesus Christ has gone ahead as a forerunner for us, and engages God Almighty on our behalf. It is for this reason alone that man may reach that for which he was created, and finally communes with the source of his being, loving the fountain of his life, praying to the One who has begotten him and resting in the knowledge that God made heaven and earth.[Q47]

Not all of the scientific facts ever assembled in any university of the world can support one spiritual fact—because you are dealing with two different realms. One deals with reason, and the other deals with faith in God.Q48

~

Almost all who preach or write on the subject of faith have much the same things to say concerning it. They tell us that it is believing a promise, that it is taking God at His word, that it is reckoning the Bible to be true and stepping out upon it. The rest of the book or sermon is usually taken up with stories of persons who have had their prayers answered as a result of their faith. These answers are mostly direct gifts of a practical and temporal nature such as health, money, physical protection or success in business. Or if the teacher is of a philosophic turn of mind he may take another course and lose us in a welter of metaphysics or snow us under with psychological jargon as he defines and redefines, paring the slender hair of faith thinner and thinner till it disappears in gossamer shavings at last. When he is finished we get up disappointed and go out "by that same door where in we went." Surely there must be something better than this.A87

~

Faith rests upon character. Faith must rest in confidence upon the One who made the promise.Q49

Forgiveness

In the Bible the offer of pardon on the part of God is conditioned upon intention to reform on the part of man. There can be no spiritual regeneration till there has been a moral reformation.^{C 42}

~

Human forgiveness is not always like God's. When a person makes a mistake and has to be forgiven, the shadow may hang over him or her because it is hard for other people to forget.

But when God forgives, He begins the new page right there, and then the devil runs up and says, "What about this person's past?" God replies, "What past? There is no past. We started out fresh when he came to Me and I forgave him!" Q115

G

Gifts/Giving

Any temporal possession can be turned into everlasting wealth. Whatever is given to Christ is immediately touched with immortality.D107

~

The Just died for the unjust; and because He did, the unjust may now live with the Just in complete moral congruity. Thanks be to God for His unspeakable gift.E49

~

God always gives us an overplus.L26

~

If I should pray for all of the spiritual gifts listed in Paul's epistles and the Spirit of God should see fit to give me all seventeen, it would be extremely dangerous for me if, in the giving, God did not give Himself, as well.M24

God

People testify that they give their tithe because God makes their nine-tenths go farther than the ten-tenths. That is not spirituality; that is just plain business. I insist that it is a dangerous thing to associate the working of God with our prosperity and success down here. I cannot promise that if you will follow the Lord you will soon experience financial prosperity, because that is not what He promised His disciples. Down through the years following the Lord has meant that we count all things but loss for the excellency of the knowledge of Christ.M73

~

Oh, yes, we do tithe! But the nine-tenths that we keep is still a hundred times more than our mothers and fathers used to have. It is right that we should tithe because it is God's work, but it does not really cost us anything—it does not bring us to the point of sacrificial giving.T70

God

We pursue God because, and only because, He has first put an urge within us that spurs us to the pursuit.A11

~

If we would find God amid all the religious externals, we must first determine to find Him, and then proceed in the way of simplicity. Now as always God discovers Himself to "babes" and hides Himself in thick darkness from the wise and the prudent. We must simplify our approach to Him. We must strip down to essentials (and they will be found to

74

be blessedly few). We must put away all effort to impress and come with the guileless candor of childhood. If we do this, without doubt God will quickly respond.[A18]

~

We need not fear that in seeking God only we may narrow our lives or restrict the motions of our expanding hearts. The opposite is true. We can well afford to make God our All, to concentrate, to sacrifice the many for the One.[A18]

~

A loving Personality dominates the Bible, walking among the trees of the garden and breathing fragrance over every scene. Always a living Person is present, speaking, pleading, loving, working and manifesting Himself whenever and wherever His people have the receptivity necessary to receive the manifestation.[A50]

~

When the habit of inwardly gazing Godward becomes fixed within us we shall be ushered onto a new level of spiritual life more in keeping with the promises of God and the mood of the New Testament. The Triune God will be our dwelling place even while our feet walk the low road of simple duty here among men.[A97]

~

God will respond to our efforts to know Him.[C 13]

God can be known satisfactorily only as we devote time to Him.C 12

~

The fellowship of God is delightful beyond all telling. He communes with His redeemed ones in an easy, uninhibited fellowship that is restful and healing to the soul. He is not sensitive nor selfish nor temperamental. What He is today we shall find Him tomorrow and the next day and the next year. He is not hard to please, though He may be hard to satisfy. He expects of us only what He has Himself first supplied. He is quick to mark every simple effort to please Him, and just as quick to overlook imperfections when He knows we meant to do His will. He loves us for ourselves and values our love more than galaxies of new created worlds.C 15

~

God is the sum of all patience and the essence of kindly good will. We please Him most, not by frantically trying to make ourselves good, but by throwing ourselves into His arms with all our imperfections and believing that He understands everything and loves us still.C 16

~

To attribute size to God is to make Him subject to degrees, which He can never be, seeing that the very idea of degree relates to created things only. That which is infinite cannot be greater or less, larger or smaller, and God is infinite. God simply is without qualification.D72

*E*verything God does is praiseworthy and deserves our deepest admiration. Whether He is making or redeeming a world, He is perfect in all His doings and glorious in all His goings forth.[E119]

~

I think it may be said with a fair degree of accuracy that all the great devotional theologians of the centuries taught the futility of trying to visualize the Godhead.[F91]

~

*D*o not try to imagine God, or you will have an imaginary God; and certainly do not, as some have done, "set a chair for Him." God is Spirit. He dwells in your heart, not your house. Brood on the Scriptures and let faith show you God as He is revealed there. Nothing else can equal this glorious sight.

God is never found accidentally. "Ye shall seek me, and find me, when ye shall search for me with all your heart" (Jeremiah 29:13).[G56]

~

*T*he holiness of God, the wrath of God and the health of the creation are inseparably united. Not only is it right for God to display anger against sin, but I find it impossible to understand how He could do otherwise.[G111]

God

Communion with God is one thing; familiarity with God is quite another thing. I don't like to hear God called "You." "You" is a colloquial expression. I can call a man "you," but I ought to call God "Thou" and "Thee." I know these are old Elizabethan words, but I also know that there are some things too precious to cast lightly away and I think that when we talk to God we ought to use the pure, respectful pronouns.K21

~

The God of the modern evangelical rarely astonishes anybody. He manages to stay pretty much within the constitution. Never breaks over our bylaws. He's a very well-behaved God and very denominational and very much one of us, and we ask Him to help us when we're in trouble and look to Him to watch over us when we're asleep. The God of the modern evangelical isn't a God I could have much respect for. But when the Holy Spirit shows us God as He is we admire Him to the point of wonder and delight.K22

~

God takes pleasure in confounding everything that comes under the guise of human power—which is really weakness disguised! Our intellectual power, our great mind, our array of talents—all of these are good if God has so ordered, but in reality they are human weaknesses disguised.M96

~

You can put all of your confidence in God. He is not angry with you, His dear child! He is not waiting to pounce on you in judgment—He knows that we are dust and He is loving and patient toward us.[M126]

~

Remember that the living God is everything. Not success, not victory—but God. Not winning, not losing—but God.[O65]

~

The God that men believe in now, the God to whom they are "sensitive," is a kind of divine Pan with a pipe who plays lovely music while they dance, but he's not a God that makes any moral demands on them.[O118]

~

Loneliness for God—you will want God so badly you will be miserable. This means you are getting close, friend. You are near the kingdom, and if you will only keep on, you will meet God. God will take you in and fill you, and He will do it in His own blessed and wonderful way.[P74]

~

God is not just a redcap, who serves you and carries your suitcase. God is God. He made heaven and earth, holds the world in His hand, measures the dust of the earth in the balance and spreads the sky out like a mantle. He is the great God Almighty—He is not your servant! He is your Father, and you are His child. He sitteth in heaven, and you are on the earth.[Q51]

God is looking for a people who want to be right.[P145]

~

God is not in our beings by Himself! He cannot do His will in us and through us because we refuse to put away the rivals. When Jesus Christ has cleansed everything from the temple and dwells there alone, He will work![R48]

~

I know that people do not want to be alone with God, but if your longing heart ever finds the living water, it will be alone. We humans want to help each other and that is good insofar as we can, but God wants us to press through to His Presence where there is no natural or artificial help. Our denominations have their place, but they cannot aid us at this point of aloneness. He asks that we come with a naked intent unto God. We must want God Himself—and nothing more![R81]

~

Jesus said there are fire and worms in hell, but that is not the reason it is hell. You might endure worms and fire, but for a moral creature to know and realize that he is where he is because he is a rebel—that is the essence of hell and judgment. It is the eternal world of all the disobedient rebels who have said, "I owe God nothing!" [S29]

God always touches with infinity everything that he does, and this leads to the thought that the inheritance we receive must be equal to the God who gives it. Being God, He does not deal in things which are merely finite. Therefore, the inheritance that the child of God receives is limitless and infinite.[S73]

~

God being who He is, the inheritance we receive from Him is limitless—it is all of the universe![S74]

~

The true Christian fears God with a trembling reverence and yet he is not afraid of God at all. He draws nigh to God with full assurance of faith and victory and yet at the same time is trembling with holy awe and fear.[S142]

~

In the kingdom of God the surest way to lose something is to try to protect it, and the best way to keep it is to let it go.[D96]

~

There are many in the churches of our day who talk some of the Christian language but who know God only by hearsay.

Most of them have read some book about God. They have seen some reflection of the light of God. They may have heard some faint echo of the voice of God, but their own personal knowledge of God is very slight.[M23]

Never can we rise to face God by what we know and by what we are, but only by love and faith are we lifted thus to know Him and adore Him!M107

~

When we begin to doubt the validity of a philosophy built on physical science and to question the soundness of a civilization that produced the H-bomb, and especially when we begin to grope after God if perchance we may find Him, something strange and wonderful happens.N13

~

We must repudiate this great, modern wave of seeking God for His benefits. The sovereign God wants to be loved for Himself and honored for Himself, but that is only part of what He wants. The other part is that He wants us to know that when we have Him, we have everything—we have all the rest.R116

~

So many are busy "using" God. Use God to get a job. Use God to give us safety. Use God to give us peace of mind. Use God to obtain success in business. Use God to provide heaven at last. R116

~

Christian believers have been going through a process of indoctrination and brainwashing, so it has become easy for us to adopt a kind of creed that makes God to be our servant instead of our being God's servant.[R116]

~

God is not silent and has never been silent, but is speaking in His universe. The written Word is effective because, and only because, the Living Word is speaking in heaven and the Living Voice is sounding in the earth. "And it is the Spirit that beareth witness, because the Spirit is truth. For there are three that bear record in heaven, the Father, the Word, and the Holy Ghost: and these three are one. And there are three that bear witness in earth, the Spirit, and the water, and the blood: and these three agree in one" (1 John 5:6-8).[N8]

The Face of God
The smiling face of God is always turned toward us—but the cloud of concealment is of our own making.[M113]

The Faithfulness of God
Upon God's faithfulness rests our whole hope of future blessedness. Only as He is faithful will His covenants stand and His promises be honored. Only as we have complete assurance that He is faithful may we live in peace and look forward with assurance to the life to come.[F81]

The Glory of God
God is always glorified when He wins a moral victory over us, and we are always benefited, immeasurably and glori-

ously benefited. The glory of God and the everlasting welfare of His people are always bound up together.C 118

The Grace of God

No man can set up the rules as to how much you can have of God. The Lord Himself has promised that as far as He is concerned He is willing to keep the candles of your soul brightly burning!R96

~

To become effective men of God, then, we must know and acknowledge that every grace and every virtue proceeds from God alone, and that not even a good thought can come from us except it be of Him.R98

~

Even in the face of man's sin and lost condition, there is still that basic potential in the soul and nature of man that through grace can become more like God than anything in the universe.M19

~

I believe in prevenient grace, and I don't believe that any person can ever be nudged or pushed or jostled into the kingdom of God or into the deeper life except the Holy Ghost does it. He does it out of the everlasting love of His Godhead, the old saint told us, "so tenderly, he would not suffer thee to be so far from him." M58

God will sift out those who only speculate about the claims of Christ and He will lead forward those who by His grace see Him in His beauty and seek Him in His love.[M79]

~

We could never have created ourselves and we could never have redeemed ourselves. We cannot talk ourselves into getting a longing for God. It has to come from God.[R36]

The Image of God
God originally created man in His own image so that man could know companionship with God in a unique sense and to a degree which is impossible for any other creature to experience.[M18]

~

Many men and women are troubled by the thought that they are too small and inconsequential in the scheme of things. But that is not our real trouble—we are actually too big and too complex, for God made us in His image and we are too big to be satisfied with what the world offers us![T170]

~

To become like God is and must be the supreme goal of all moral creatures. This is the reason for their creation, the end apart from which no excuse can be found for their existence. Leaving out of consideration for the moment those strange and beautiful heavenly beings of which we have hints in the Bible but about which we know so little, we concentrate upon the fallen race of mankind. Once made in the image of God we kept not our first estate, but left our proper habitation, consorted with Satan and walked according to the course of this world, according to the prince of the power of the air, the spirit that now worketh in the children of disobedience. But God who is rich in mercy, for His great love wherewith He loved us even when we were dead in sins, provided atonement for us . . . the purpose being stated in Romans 8:29: "For whom he did foreknow, he also did predestinate to be conformed to the image of his Son."[N197]

The Love of God

There is a place in the religious experience where we love God for Himself alone, with never a thought of His benefits.[C 149]

∼

Before we were born, God was God, the Lord God Almighty! He has never needed us. None of our human talents and abilities are significant to Him. But He needs our love and wants our love![M145]

∼

The only eccentricity that I can discover in the heart of God is that a God such as He is should love sinners such as we are![R101]

God's love shed abroad in our hearts—compassion and love which can only be found in Jesus Christ, our Lord—these are the only elements of true unity among men and women today. All other emphasis on unity is a sadly strange and ironic joke that must have had its origin in the seventh hell below![U114]

~

The Bible pictures God as a very careful, tenderhearted Father, busying Himself about the troubles of His people. He looks after them, goes ahead of them, cares for them and guides them all the way through.

There you see the problem of worry and anxiety is solved by the assurance that while there are things about which to be concerned, why should you worry, when Somebody is taking care of you![O131]

~

The result of what God saw among men was grief to God's own heart . . . and only love can grieve. You cannot grieve unless you love. God loved the man whom He had made and the degenerate and corrupt race that had descended from Him. God's love caused Him to grieve, and it filled Him with anxious care.[P137]

The Mercy of God

If we have life, it is according to the mercy of God. If we have protection, it is according to the mercy of God. If we have food and sustenance, it is of God's mercy. If we have providence to guide us, it is surely in the mercy of God.[S46]

God blesses us because of His abundant mercy, the mercy which He has bestowed upon us, and not because of any of our goodness. I do not believe that heaven itself will ever permit us to forget that we are recipients of the goodness of God and for that reason I do not believe that you and I will ever be permitted to forget Calvary.[S55]

~

We do believe in justice and we do believe in judgment. We believe the only reason mercy triumphs over judgment is that God, by a divine, omniscient act of redemption, fixed it so man could escape justice and live in the sea of mercy. The justified man, the man who believes in Jesus Christ, born anew and now a redeemed child of God, lives in that mercy always.[S55]

The Omnipresence of God

The great God Almighty who fills the universe and over-flows into immensity can never be surrounded by that little thing that we call our brain, our mind, our intellect—never, never, never! Never can we rise to face God by what we know and by what we are, but only by love and faith are we lifted thus to know Him and adore Him![R82]

~

We do not need any enlarging adjectives when we speak of God or of His love or mercy. God Almighty fills the universe and overfills it because it is His character—infinite and unlimited![S50]

God

We habitually stand in our *now* and look back by faith to see the past filled with God. We look forward and see Him inhabiting our future; but our *now* is uninhabited except for ourselves. Thus we are guilty of a kind of pro tem atheism which leaves us alone in the universe while, for the time, God is not. We talk of Him much and loudly, but we secretly think of Him as being absent, and we think of ourselves as inhabiting a parenthetic interval between the God who was and the God who will be. And we are lonely with an ancient and cosmic loneliness.[B23]

~

God is always first, and God will surely be last.

To say this is not to draw God downward into the stream of time and involve Him in the flux and flow of the world. He stands above His own creation and outside of time; but for the convenience of His creatures, who are children of time, He makes free use of time-words when referring to Himself. So He says that He is Alpha and Omega, the beginning and the ending, the first and the last.[C 158]

~

God is always previous. God is always there first, and if you have any desire for God and for the things of God, it is God Himself who put it there.[M57]

~

With God Abram's day and this day are the same.[B28]

The first announcement of God's redemptive intention toward mankind was made to a man and a woman hiding in mortal fear from the presence of the Lord.C 38

~

At the risk of being written off as an extremist or a borderline fanatic we offer it as our mature opinion that more spiritual progress can be made in one short moment of speechless silence in the awesome presence of God than in years of mere study.C 146

~

It is not so important that we know all of the history and all of the scientific facts, but it is vastly important that we desire and know and cherish the Presence of the Living God, who has given Jesus Christ to be the propitiation for our sins—and not for ours only, but also for the sins of the whole world. 117

The Purpose of God

Everything that God does in His ransomed children has as its long-range purpose the final restoration of the divine image in human nature. Everything looks forward to the consummation.C 60

~

God never acts without purpose—never. People act without purpose. . . . A great deal of what we do in the church today is purposeless. But God never acts without a purpose. Intellect is an attribute of the deity. God has intellect and this means that God thinks; and so God never does anything without an intelligent purpose. Nothing in this world is without meaning.[K1]

~

God put the universe together with a purpose and there isn't a single useless thing anywhere, not any spare parts; everything fits into everything else. God made it like that. Science of course deals with the relation of things and their effect upon each other. But the plain people, the simple people, the people who would rather believe than to know, and who would rather worship than to discover—they have a simpler and a more beautiful view of the world. They say that in the beginning God created the heavens and the earth, and that God made everything and put it in its place and gave it meaning and purpose and a task to fulfill in relation to all other things which He also made.[K1]

~

But God saw that the world wasn't complete, so as the poem has it, this great God who threw the stars into the sky and made the sun and holds all the universe in His hand, this great God stooped down by the riverbank and took a piece of clay and, like a mammy bending over her baby, He worked on this clay until it became a man and into it He blew the breath of life and it became a living soul. Amen! Amen! That's what we believe. We don't think about it in quite such a physical way as that, but we believe that God in His intelligence created the universe with intelligent purpose back of it.[K2]

God made man for a purpose and that purpose is given by the catechism; the answer is, "To glorify God and to enjoy Him forever." God made us to be worshipers. That was the purpose of God in bringing us into the world.[K3]

~

God seeks out those who are willing that their lives should be fashioned according to His own grace and love. He sifts out those who cannot see God's purpose and design for our blessing.[M80]

The Will of God
The will of God is always best, whatever the circumstances, and Jesus refused the crown and took the cross deliberately because that was in the will of God, both for Him and for humankind.[Q153]

~

The will of God is one thing but to have the will of God is another.[R80]

~

That is the only right we have here—to make our wills the wills of God, to make the will of God our will![S25]

Yet for all God's good will toward us He is unable to grant us our heart's desires till all our desires have been reduced to one.D10

~

We urgently need a new kind of reformation throughout our Christian churches—a reformation that will cause us not only to accept the will of God but to actively seek it and adore it!M89

God and Man

God made us for Himself—that is the only explanation that satisfies the *heart* of a thinking man, whatever his wild reason may say.A33

~

God formed us for His pleasure, and so formed us that we, as well as He, can in divine communion enjoy the sweet and mysterious mingling of kindred personalities. He meant us to see Him and live with Him and draw our life from His smile.A34

~

A spiritual kingdom lies all about us, enclosing us, embracing us, altogether within reach of our inner selves, waiting for us to recognize it. God Himself is here waiting our response to His presence. This eternal world will come alive to us the moment we begin to reckon upon its reality.[A52]

~

What God in His sovereignty may yet do on a world-scale I do not claim to know. But what He will do for the plain man or woman who seeks His face I believe I do know and can tell others. Let any man turn to God in earnest, let him begin to exercise himself unto godliness, let him seek to develop his powers of spiritual receptivity by trust and obedience and humility, and the results will exceed anything he may have hoped in his leaner and weaker days.[A70]

~

The cause of all our human miseries is a radical moral dislocation, an upset in our relation to God and to each other.[A99]

~

Every soul belongs to God and exists by His pleasure. God being who and what He is, and we being who and what we are, the only thinkable relation between us is one of full Lordship on His part and complete submission on ours. We owe Him every honor that it is in our power to give Him. Our everlasting grief lies in giving Him anything less.[A102]

The man of God set his heart to exalt God above all; God accepted his intention as fact and acted accordingly. Not perfection, but holy intention made the difference.[A106]

~

The whole course of the life is upset by failure to put God where He belongs.[A107]

~

In our desire after God let us keep always in mind that God also has desire, and His desire is toward the sons of men, and more particularly toward those sons of men who will make the once-for-all decision to exalt Him over all.[A107]

~

The whole man must make the decision before the heart can know any real satisfaction. God wants the whole person, and He will not rest till He gets us in entirety. No part of the man will do.[A107]

~

The degree of blessing enjoyed by any man will correspond exactly with the completeness of God's victory over him.[B53]

Human personality is dear to God because it is of all created things the nearest to being like Himself.C 98

～

To speak to God on behalf of men is probably the highest service any of us can render. The next is to speak to men in the name of God. Either is a privilege possible to us only through the grace of our Lord Jesus Christ.D3

～

Only that creature whom He called "man" did God make in His own image and likeness. So, when man failed and sinned and fell, God said, "I will go down now."

God came down to visit us in the form of a man, for in Jesus Christ we have the incarnation, "God manifest in the flesh." God Himself came down to this earthly island of man's grief and assumed our loss and took upon Himself our demerits, and in so doing redeemed us back unto Himself. Jesus Christ, the King of glory, the everlasting Son of the Father, in His victory over sin and death opened the kingdom of heaven to all believers!

That is what the Bible teaches. That is what the Christian church believes. It is the essence of the doctrines of the Christian church relating to atonement and salvation.T108

～

The man that has the most of God is the man who is seeking the most ardently for more of God.G106

The teaching of the New Testament is that now, at this very moment, there is a man in heaven appearing in the presence of God for us. He is as certainly a man as was Adam or Moses or Paul. He is a man glorified, but His glorification did not dehumanize Him. Today He is a real man, of the race of mankind, bearing our lineaments and dimensions, a visible and audible man whom any other man would recognize instantly as one of us.[G142]

~

When God resists a man for the sins of his spirit and attitude, a slow, inward spiritual degeneration will take place as a signal of the judgment that has come. A slow hardening that comes from unwillingness to yield will result in cynicism. The Christian joy will disappear and there will be no more fruits of the Spirit.[H101]

~

Men and women have lost all sight of the fact that they are important to God. We are all important to God in setting forth the glory of the Lord Jesus Christ.[I160]

~

Man is bored, because he is too big to be happy with that which sin is giving him. God has made him too great, his potential is too mighty. [I170]

Good/Evil

God wants to humble you and fill you with Himself and control you so that you can become part of the eternal work that God wants to do in the earth in your day! J41

~

Man is better qualified to appreciate God than any other creature because he was made in His image and is the only creature who was. This admiration for God grows and grows until it fills the heart with wonder and delight. K22

Good/Evil

The man who wants to do the right thing and does it because he wants to do it is a good man! Q101

~

You can be as good as you want to and yet go to hell if you have not put your trust in Jesus Christ! The devil is not going to waste his time causing any trouble for the preacher whose only message is, "Be good!" T142

~

If a man's will is not free to do evil, it is not free to do good!
    The freedom of human will is necessary to the concept of morality. J87

98

There has never been a time in history when people were good, but there have been times when the masses were ashamed of being bad. We have now degenerated to the point where we make belly-laughing jokes out of our evil ways and our scandalous morals. . . .

When the moral philosophy of a whole generation becomes such that people can flaunt their evil and rottenness and wind up being celebrated on the front pages of our newspapers, then God will withhold His hand no longer.

We will rot from within. When we say this is the desert, we have our facts before us. The desert is all about us.[Q129]

Greatness

True greatness lies in character, not in ability or position.[D50]

~

The great men of the earth are still only men. [I63]

H

Healing/Health

There have always been reverent, serious men who felt it their sacred duty to pray for the sick that they might be healed in the will of God. . . . When tearless promoters took up the doctrine it was turned into a lucrative racket. Smooth, persuasive men used superior salesmanship methods to make impressive fortunes out of their campaigns. Their big ranches and heavy financial investments prove how success-ful they have been in separating the sick and suffering from their money. And this in the name of the Man of Sorrows who had not where to lay His head![N10]

~

Healing is for us today. Whatever God did and was able to do and willing to do at any time, God is able and willing to do again, within the framework of His will!

So what we need to do is get acquainted with God.[O34]

The Heart

Truth engages the citadel of the human heart and is not sat-isfied until it has conquered everything there.[E27]

Keep your heart open to the correction of the Lord and be ready to receive His chastisement regardless of who holds the whip.C 30

~

The Spirit of God never promised to fill a man's head. The promise is that God will fill the heart or man's innermost being.M101

~

The human heart is idolatrous and will worship anything it can possess. Therein lies the danger of the "good" things. We have surrendered evil things, bad things, but we hold on to the good things and these we are prone to worship. Whatever we refuse to surrender and count but loss we will ultimately worship. It may be something good, but it gets between you and God—whether it be property or family or reputation or security or your life itself.R46

~

The things that are closest to our hearts are the things we talk about, and if God is close to your heart, you will talk about Him!O31

Heaven/Hell

We must face today as children of tomorrow. We must meet

the uncertainties of this world with the certainty of the world to come. To the pure in heart nothing really bad can happen. He may die, but what is death to a Christian? Not death but sin should be our great fear. Without doubt the heavens being on fire shall be dissolved, and the earth and the works that are therein shall be burned up. Sooner or later that will come. But what of it? Do not we, according to His promise, look for new heavens and a new earth, wherein dwelleth righteousness?E132

~

We have come to a wretched emphasis in the Christian Church, so that when we talk about the future, we talk about "eschatology" instead of heaven.

Once more I repeat that Christians are living too much in the "present now"—and the anticipation of better things to come has almost died out of the Church of Christ.

We find ourselves so well-situated now that we don't really need any tomorrow's heaven. We don't need to hope— we have everything well enough now.O150

~

The merits of Jesus are enough! We are going to heaven on the merits of another—there is no question about that. We will get in because another went out on our behalf. We will live because another died. We will be with God because another was rejected from the presence of God in the terror of the crucifixion. We go to heaven on the merits of another.Q55

There are many legal reasons why I should not go to heaven. There are governmental reasons why I should not go to heaven. I believe that a holy God must run His universe according to holy law—and I do not belong there because I have broken every one of those holy laws in some way. Therefore, there has to be a redemption, a justification of some kind if I am to have God and He is to have me.

Thank God, it has been done! The New Testament language is plain as can be—in Jesus Christ and through His death and resurrection every legal hindrance has been met and taken away. There is nothing to stop you except yourself—no reason why we cannot enter into all the depths of the fullness of God![R82]

~

If there is grief in heaven, I think it must come from the fact that we want God's gifts, but we don't want God Himself as our environment.[R115]

~

Heaven is the world of God's obedient children. Whatever else we may say of its pearly gates, its golden streets and its jasper walls, heaven is heaven because it is the world of obedient children. Heaven is heaven because children of the Most High God find they are in their normal sphere as obedient moral beings.[S29]

~

When the followers of Jesus Christ lose their interest in heaven they will no longer be happy Christians, and when they are no longer happy Christians they cannot be a powerful force in a sad and sinful world. It may be said with certainty that Christians who have lost their enthusiasm about the Savior's promises of heaven-to-come have also stopped being effective in Christian life and witness in this world.[T105]

~

It is hard indeed to focus attention upon a better world to come when a more comfortable one than this can hardly be imagined. As long as science can make us so cozy in this present world it is admittedly hard to work up much pleasurable anticipation of a new world order even if it is God who has promised it.[U152]

~

Ours is the age in which Christ has been explained, humanized, demoted. Many professing Christians no longer expect Him to usher in a new order. They are not at all sure that He is able to do so; or if He does, it will be with the help of art, education, science and technology—that is, with the help of man.[U152]

~

He is longsuffering and waits patiently to be gracious, but after a while the friendly invitation of the gospel is withdrawn. The effort to persuade the incorrigible sinner is discontinued, death fixes the status of the man who loved his sins and he is sent to the place of the rejected where there is for him no further hope. That is hell, and it may be well we

know so little about it. What we do know is sufficiently terrifying.[N41]

Holiness

The whole purpose of God in redemption is to make us holy
and to restore us to the image of God. To accomplish this
He disengages us from earthly ambitions and draws us away
from the cheap and unworthy prizes that worldly men set
their hearts upon.[C 25]

~

The true Christian ideal is not to be happy but to be
holy.[B100]

~

No man should desire to be happy who is not at the same
time holy. He should spend his efforts in seeking to know
and do the will of God, leaving to Christ the matter of how
happy he shall be.[E46]

~

The more we learn of God and His ways and of man and
his nature we are bound to reach the conclusion that we are
all just about as holy as we want to be. We are all just about
as full of the Spirit as we want to be. Thus when we tell ourselves that we want to be more holy but we are really as holy

as we care to be, it is small wonder that the dark night of the soul takes so long![R57]

Holy Spirit

Most Christians are not joyful persons because they are not holy persons, and they are not holy persons because they are not filled with the Holy Spirit, and they are not filled with the Holy Spirit because they are not separated persons.

The Spirit cannot fill whom He cannot separate, and whom He cannot fill, He cannot make holy, and whom He cannot make holy, He cannot make happy![R12]

~

When the Spirit presents Christ to our inner vision it has an exhilarating effect on the soul much as wine has on the body. The Spirit-filled man may literally dwell in a state of spiritual fervor amounting to a mild and pure inebriation.[E9]

~

I have heard the notion seriously advanced that whereas once to win men to Christ it was necessary to have a gift from the Holy Spirit, now religious movies make it possible for anyone to win souls, without such spiritual anointing! "Whom the gods would destroy they first make mad." Surely such a notion is madness, but until now I have not heard it challenged among the evangelicals.[G65]

Many Christians spend a lot of time and energy in making excuses, because they have never broken through into a real offensive for God by the unlimited power of the Holy Spirit![H34]

~

All of us who love our Lord Jesus Christ are facing such great changes in this period before the return of Christ that we are going to have to recall and have back upon us the kind of spiritual revival that will eventuate in a new moral power, in a new spirit of willing separation and heart purity and a new bestowing of the enablings of the Spirit of God.[J67]

~

The Holy Spirit is a Being dwelling in another mode of existence. He has not weight, nor measure, nor size, nor any color, nor extension in space, but He nevertheless exists as surely as you exist.[L11]

~

The Holy Spirit is not enthusiasm. I have found enthusiasm that hummed with excitement, and the Holy Spirit was nowhere to be found there at all; and I have found the Holy Spirit when there has not been much of what we call enthusiasm present.[L11]

The Holy Spirit has will and intelligence and feeling and knowledge and sympathy and ability to love and see and think and hear and speak and desire the same as any person has.[L12]

~

There is an unseen Deity present, a knowing, feeling Personality, and He is indivisible from the Father and the Son, so that if you were to be suddenly transferred to heaven itself you wouldn't be any closer to God than you are now, for God is already here. Changing your geographical location would not bring you any nearer to God nor God any nearer to you, because the indivisible Trinity is present, and all that the Son is the Holy Ghost is, and all that the Father is the Holy Ghost is, and the Holy Ghost is in His Church.[L20]

~

Nobody ever need to be afraid of Jesus, because He is the epitome of love, kindliness, geniality, warm attractiveness and sweetness. And that is exactly what the Holy Ghost is, for He is the Spirit of the Father and the Son. Amen.[L21]

~

The Holy Spirit came to carry the evidence of Christianity from the book of apologetics into the human heart.[L28]

The Spirit gave a bright, emotional quality to their religion, and I grieve before my God over the lack of this in our day. The emotional quality isn't there. There is a sickliness about us all; we pump so hard trying to get a little drop of delight out of our old rusty well, and we write innumerable bouncy choruses, and we pump and pump until you can hear the old rusty thing squeak across 40 acres. But it doesn't work.

Then He gave them direct spiritual authority. By that I mean He removed their fears, their questions, their apologies and their doubts, and they had an authority that was founded upon life.L31

~

The Spirit-filled life is not a special, deluxe edition of Christianity. It is part and parcel of the total plan of God for His people.L39

~

The Holy Spirit is a living Person. He is the third Person of the Trinity. He is Himself God, and as a Person, He can be cultivated; He can be wooed and cultivated the same as any person can be. People grow on us, and the Holy Spirit, being a Person, can grow on us.L53

~

The only power God recognizes in His church is the power of His Spirit whereas the only power actually recognized today by the majority of evangelicals is the power of man. God does His work by the operation of the Spirit, while Christian leaders attempt to do theirs by the power of trained and devoted intellect. Bright personality has taken the place of the divine afflatus.

Everything that men do in their own strength and by means of their own abilities is done for time alone; the quality of eternity is not in it. Only what is done through the Eternal Spirit will abide eternally; all else is wood, hay, stubble.N111

~

Wherever Jesus is glorified, the Holy Spirit comes!P10

~

The Spirit is faithful in His message that the restoration of the Spirit of God to His rightful place in the church and in the life of the believer is by all means the most important thing that could possibly take place.

If you could increase the attendance of your church until there is no more room, if you could provide everything they have in churches that men want and love and value, and yet you didn't have the Holy Spirit, you might as well have nothing at all. For, " 'Not by might nor by power, but by my Spirit,' says the LORD Almighty" (Zechariah 4:6, NIV). Not by the eloquence of a man, not by good music, not by good preaching, but it is by the Spirit that God works His mighty works.P38

~

Spell this out in capital letters: THE HOLY SPIRIT IS A PERSON. He is not enthusiasm. He is not courage. He is not energy. He is not the personification of all good qualities like Jack Frost is the personification of cold weather. Actually, the Holy Spirit is not the personification of anything. He is a Person, just the same as you are a person, and He has all the qualities of a person. He has substance but not material substance. He has individuality. He is one being and not another. He has will and intelligence. He has hearing. He has knowledge and sympathy and ability to love and see and think. He can hear, speak, desire, grieve and rejoice. He is a Person.

The Holy Spirit can communicate with you and can love you. He can be grieved when you resist and ignore Him. He can be quenched as any friend can be shut up if you turn on him when he is in your home as a guest. Of course, He will be hushed into hurt silence if you wound Him, and we can wound the Holy Spirit.P42

~

The Holy Spirit is God, and the most important thing is that the Holy Spirit is present now. There is unseen deity present. I cannot bring Him to you; I can only tell you that He is here. I can tell you that He is present in our midst, a knowing, feeling personality.

He knows how you are reacting to the truth of His being and personality and presence. He knows what you are thinking now. You cannot hide from Him—He is present now. Jesus said, "[The Father] will give you another Counselor to be with you forever" (John 14:16, NIV). So He is here among us now. He is indivisible from the Father and the Son, and He is all God and exercises all the rights of God and He merits all worship and all love and all obedience. That's who the Holy Spirit is!P46

The body of Christians is carnal. The Lord's people ought to be a sanctified, pure, clean people, but we are a carnal crowd. We are carnal in our attitudes, in our tastes and carnal in many things. Our young people often are not reverent in our Christian services. We have so degraded our religious tastes that our Christian service is largely exhibitionism. We desperately need a divine visitation—for our situation will never be cured by sermons! It will never be cured until the Church of Christ has suddenly been confronted with what one man called the "mysterium tremendium"—the fearful mystery that is God, the fearful majesty that is God. This is what the Holy Ghost does. He brings the wonderful mystery that is God to us, and presents Him to the human spirit.P60

~

We will never know more about God than the Spirit teaches us. We will never know any more about Jesus than the Spirit teaches us, because there is only the Spirit to do the teaching. O Holy Ghost, how we have grieved Thee! How we have insulted Thee! How we have rejected Thee!

He is our Teacher, and if He does not teach us, we never can know. He is our Illuminator, and if He does not turn on the light, we never can see. He is the Healer of our deaf ears, and if He does not touch our ears, we never can hear. Churches can run for weeks and months and years without knowing anything about this or having the Spirit of the living God fall upon them. Oh, my heart, be still before Him, prostrate, inwardly adore Him!P61

~

We have the blessed Holy Spirit present, and we are treating Him as if He were not present at all.

We resist Him, disobey Him, quench Him and compromise with our hearts. We hear a sermon about Him and determine to learn more and do something about it. Our conviction wears off, and soon we go back to the same old dead level we were in before. We resist the blessed Comforter. He has come to comfort. He has come to teach. He is the Spirit of instruction. He has come to bring light for He is the Spirit of light. He comes to bring purity for He is the Spirit of holiness. He comes to bring power for He is the Spirit of power.[P62]

~

The Holy Spirit is pure, for He is the Holy Spirit. He is wise, for He is the Spirit of wisdom. He is true, for He is the Spirit of truth. He is like Jesus, for He is the Spirit of Christ. He is like the Father, for He is the Spirit of the Father. He wants to be the Lord of your life, and He wants to possess you so that you are no longer in command of the little vessel in which you sail. You may be a passenger on board, or one of the crew, but you definitely are not in charge. Someone else is in command of the vessel.[P68]

~

We would like to be full of the Spirit and yet go on and do as we please. The Holy Spirit who inspired the Scriptures will expect obedience to the Scriptures, and if we do not obey the Scriptures, we will quench Him. This Spirit will have obedience—but people do not want to obey the Lord. Everyone is as full as he wants to be. Everyone has as much of God as he desires to have. There is a fugitive impulse that comes to us, in spite of what we ask for when we pray in public, or even in private. We want the thrill of being full, but we don't want to meet the conditions. We just don't want to be filled badly enough to be filled.[P68]

~

If there is anything in your life more demanding than your longing after God, then you will never be a Spirit-filled Christian.

I have met Christians who have been wanting to be filled, in a vague sort of way, for many years. The reason they have not been filled with the Spirit is because they have other things they want more. God does not come rushing into a human heart unless He knows that He is the answer and fulfillment to the greatest, most overpowering desire of that life.[P72]

~

If you will set aside the necessary time to search the Scriptures with an honest and open being, you will be convinced that fruitfulness and joy and peace and blessing and contentment are all part and parcel of what the Holy Spirit expects to provide in and through the yielded life of the Christian believer.[P80]

~

If we are not filled with the Spirit unless we have the evidence of tongues, then Augustine, Bernard, Thomas à Kempis, Frederick Faber, Charles Finney, David Livingstone, Charles Spurgeon and George Mueller weren't filled with the Holy Ghost. Not one of them ever said anything about the evidence of tongues.[P104]

Contrary to what professing Christians like to think, many of God's people are not willing to walk in perfect agreement with Him, and this may explain why so many believers do not have the power of the Spirit, the peace of the Spirit and many of the other qualities, gifts and benefits which the Spirit of God brings.[P107]

~

God Almighty is saying to us, "I am not wanting to wake up the power that lies in you. Ye shall receive the power of the Holy Spirit coming upon you!" That is a different thing altogether. If we had only to be awakened, the Lord would simply have gone around waking us up—but we need more than this. We need to be endued with power from on high.[P124]

~

The Holy Spirit is in some measure resident in the breast of everybody that's converted. Otherwise, there wouldn't be conversion. The Holy Spirit doesn't stand outside a man and regenerate him; He comes in to regenerate him. That is one thing, and we're glad and grateful for that, but it's quite another thing for the Holy Spirit to come down with His wings outspread, uninhibited, free and pleased to fill lives and to fill churches and to fill denominations. That's quite another thing.[P140]

~

I have to tell the truth, and the truth is not very well received, even by the saints. The simple truth is that unless we have a lighting down upon evangelicalism, upon fundamentalism, upon our gospel churches, unless the Dove of God can come down with His wings outspread and make Himself known and felt among us, that which is fundamentalism will be liberalism in years to come. And liberalism will be unitarianism.P141

~

The Spirit is seeking a rest for the sole of His foot. He is seeking it, and I hear the fluttering of holy wings, and I hear the mourning sound of Him who is grieved and quenched. I see Him looking about for signs of repentance, for signs of sorrow of heart and the lifting of the judgment of God from the Church. When God judges the world, it will be terror and fire, but God wants to judge the Church. He wants to judge you and me—His children. He wants to begin at the house of the Lord, and He wants to begin to judge us, and the absence of the full power of the Holy Ghost is perpetual condemnation.P142

~

Conversion is a miraculous act of God by the Holy Ghost; it must be wrought in the spirit. The body of truth, the inspired text, is not enough—there must be an inward illumination!Q16

~

There are too many who want the Holy Spirit in order that they may have the gift of healing. Others want the Holy Spirit for the gift of tongues. Others want Him to help them in the preaching ministry. Still others seek the Spirit that their testimony may become effective.

All of these things, I grant you, are a part of the total pattern of the New Testament, but it is impossible for us to make God our servant, and let us never pray that we may be filled with the Spirit of God for a secondary purpose. God wants to fill you with His Spirit as an end in your moral life. The purpose of God is that we should know Him first of all, and be lost in Him and that we should enter into the fullness of the Spirit that His Son may be glorified in us.Q156

~

The wonderful thing about the invitation of the Holy Spirit of God is that He doesn't say different things to different people. The Holy Spirit does not say two things—He says one thing! He says the same thing to all who are listening to Him.R83

~

The Holy Spirit is the gentle Dove of God and His coming to us in blessing and power is without pain or strain. The painful part is the necessity of our own preparation—for the Holy Spirit will search us out completely and deal with us solemnly.

He will guide us in necessary confessions that we must make. He will guide us in the necessity of pouring out all of that which is selfish and unlike Jesus in our lives. He will guide us in getting straightened out with people with whom we have had differences. He will guide us in seeking forgiveness where it is necessary and He will show us the necessity of old-fashioned restitution and restoration in our willingness to be a clean vessel.U103

The Church has been propagated by the Holy Spirit, so we can only worship in the Spirit, we can only pray in the Spirit, and we can only preach effectively in the Spirit, and what we do must be done by the power of the Spirit.[K14]

~

The New Testament knows nothing of the working of the Spirit in us apart from our own moral responses.[F54]

Hope

Hope is a word which has taken on a new and deeper meaning for us because the Savior took it into His mouth. Loving Him and obeying Him, we suddenly discover that hope is really the direction taken by the whole Bible. Hope is the music of the whole Bible, the heartbeat, the pulse and the atmosphere of the whole Bible.[S40]

~

Hope means a desirable expectation, a pleasurable anticipation. As men know this word, it often blows up in our faces and often cruelly disappoints us as human beings. Hope that is only human will throw us down and wound us just as pleasurable anticipation often turns to discouragement or sorrow.[S40]

We have been born of God and our Christian hope is a valid hope! No emptiness, no vanity, no dreams that cannot come true. Your expectation should rise and you should challenge God and begin to dream high dreams of faith and spiritual attainment and expect God to meet them. You cannot out-hope God and you cannot out-expect God. Remember that all of your hopes are finite, but all of God's ability is infinite![S43]

~

Your Christian hope is just as good as Jesus Christ. Your anticipation for the future lives or dies with Jesus. If He is who He said He was, you can spread your wings and soar.[S43]

Humility

It is most important for believers to acknowledge the fact that because Christ Jesus came to the world clothed in humility, He will always be found among those who are clothed with humility. He will be found among the humble people.[H98]

~

True humility is a healthy thing. The humble man accepts the truth about himself. He believes that in his fallen nature dwells no good thing. He acknowledges that apart from God he is nothing, has nothing, knows nothing and can do nothing. But this knowledge does not discourage him, for he knows also that in Christ he is somebody. He knows that he is dearer to God than the apple of His eye and that he can do all things through Christ who strengthens him; that is, he can do all that lies within the will of God for him to do.[N171]

~

The believer knows that in himself he is nothing, but even while he is humbly telling the Lord that he is nothing, he knows very well that he is the apple of God's eye![S142]

~

Many Christians are tempted to downgrade themselves too much. I am not arguing against true humility and my word to you in this: Think as little of yourself as you want to, but always remember that our Lord Jesus Christ thought very highly of you—enough to give Himself for you in death and sacrifice.[T138]

9

Idol/Idolatry

The human heart is idolatrous and will worship anything it can possess.[M70]

~

We have surrendered evil things, bad things, but we hold on to the good things and these we are prone to worship.[M69]

~

We are allowing too many rivals of God. We actually have too many gods. We have too many irons in the fire. We have too much theology that we don't understand. We have too much churchly institutionalism. We have too much religion. Actually, I guess we just have too much of too much![M71]

~

God is not in our beings by Himself! He cannot do His will in us and through us because we refuse to put away the rivals. When Jesus Christ has cleansed everything from the temple and dwells there alone, He will work![M72]

If you spend time examining your Christian brother, you will find him lacking in some things. Don't forget that all idols have feet of clay.[M140]

J

Joy/Happiness

There are delights which the heart may enjoy in the awe-some presence of God which cannot find expression in lan-guage; they belong to the unutterable element in Christian experience. Not many enjoy them because not many know that they can. The whole concept of ineffable worship has been lost to this generation of Christians.C 145

~

There also seems to be a chilling fear of holy enthusiasm among the people of God. We try to tell how happy we are—but we remain so well controlled that there are very few waves of glory experienced in our midst.M13

~

It is probably quite generally true that any Christian who has not been filled with the Spirit since his conversion does not have genuine, Christian joy. I know this was my experi-ence. I had a lot of joyful feeling when I was first converted. I was a happy Christian. But if this is the kind of happiness that is about half carnality, just animal spirits, God will want to deliver you from it. To be filled with the Spirit of God is to have come through feelings, disturbance, anxiety, disappointment and emptiness. When you reach that place of despair, when you have gone to the last person and you have written the last editor, when you have followed the last evangelist around and hunted up the last fellow to counsel with you—when no man can help you anymore and you are in a state of inward despair—that is when you will recognize that you are near the place where God can finally do what He wants to do for you. When there comes that despair with self, that emptying out of you and that inner loneliness, you are getting close.P73

~

The Lord's people are like little children—they just want to be happy. They want the Lord to give them a rattle and let them cackle and laugh and be happy. They are going to be happy regardless but the Lord's happy little children very seldom get filled with the Holy Ghost. God cannot fill them because they are not ready to die to the things upon which they have put their own values. God wants His children to be joyful, but that is not the cheap happiness of the flesh—it is the joy of a resurrected Christ!P73

~

It is part of my belief that God wants to get us to a place where we would still be happy if we had only Him! We don't need God and something else. God does give us Himself and lets us have other things, too, but there is that inner loneliness until we reach the place where it is only God that we desire.P73

*T*he reason we have to search for so many things to cheer us up is the fact that we are not really joyful and contentedly happy within.[U77]

Knowledge

A child five years old may properly be said to be educated in that he has by observation gathered a few facts and arranged them into some sort of orderly pattern within his mind. A doctor of philosophy has done nothing different; he has only gone a little further.[G146]

~

Don't throw your head away—you are going to need it! I am convinced that God has made it plain that man alone, of all the creatures on earth, is created so that he can have fullness of knowledge about the earth and all the wonders and glories that it holds. I believe that through grace man can have a fullness of knowledge even about the works of God—but this certainly does not mean that we find Him and know Him and love Him through thought processes and human wisdom.

It is utterly and completely futile to try to think our way through to knowing God, who is beyond our power of thought or visualization. This does not mean that it is impossible for us to think about Him—but it does mean that we cannot think around Him or think equal to Him or think up to Him![R77]

The best and easiest way to find out that you are no good is to have God flash that knowledge suddenly into your soul.[M127]

~

I have no doubt that historians will conclude that we of the twentieth century had intelligence enough to create a great civilization but not the moral wisdom to preserve it.[O113]

~

I know that there is an intellectual element in the gospel, for one of the attributes of deity is intellect. We call this element theology or doctrine. Human thought may engage theology, and it may engage doctrine. These things are necessary and right in their place, but there must be a seeking of the heart and being which is beyond the intellect.[R78]

~

Knowledge is the raw material out of which that finest of all machines, the mind, creates its amazing world.[G146]

L

Liberty/Freedom

The casual indifference with which millions of Protestants view their God-blessed religious liberty is ominous. Being let go they go on weekends to the lakes and mountains and beaches to play shuffleboard, fish and sunbathe. They go where their heart is and come back to the praying company only when the bad weather drives them in. Let this continue long enough and evangelical Protestantism will be ripe for a takeover by Rome.[G160]

~

Freedom is liberty within bounds: liberty to obey holy laws, liberty to keep the commandments of Christ, to serve mankind, to develop to the full all the latent possibilities within our redeemed natures. True Christian liberty never sets us free to indulge our lusts or to follow our fallen impulses.[N185]

~

Unqualified freedom in any area of human life is deadly. In government it is anarchy, in domestic life, free love and in religion, antinomianism. The freest cells in the body are cancer cells, but they kill the organism where they grow.[N186]

*T*he ideal Christian is one who knows he is free to do as he will and *wills* to be a servant. This is the path Christ took; blessed is the man who follows Him.N189

~

I can make a case for the doctrine that you cannot have morality unless you have freedom. There is a good, sound philosophy underneath it, that you cannot even have an idea of morality unless you also have freedom.

For, just as soon as we coerce a human will, that human will can be neither good nor bad—that will cannot do righteousness as long as it is coerced into it.

And the human will, driven to anything, is not doing it freely, and therefore is not doing it morally.O83

Life/Death

*W*e might well pray for God to invade and conquer us, for until He does, we remain in peril from a thousand foes. We bear within us the seeds of our own disintegration. Our moral imprudence puts us always in danger of accidental or reckless self-destruction. The strength of our flesh is an ever-present danger to our souls. Deliverance can come to us only by the defeat of our old life. Safety and peace come only after we have been forced to our knees. God rescues us by breaking us, by shattering our strength and wiping out our resistance. Then He invades our natures with that ancient and eternal life which is from the beginning. So He conquers us and by that benign conquest saves us for Himself.B57

Who but someone very old and very conservative would insist upon death as the appointed way to life? And who today is interested in a gloomy mysticism that would sentence its flesh to a cross and recommend self-effacing humility as a virtue actually to be practiced by modern Christians?[B60]

~

The life that halts short of the cross is but a fugitive and condemned thing, doomed at last to be lost beyond recovery. That life which goes to the cross and loses itself there to rise again with Christ is a divine and deathless treasure. Over it death hath no more dominion. Whoever refuses to bring his old life to the cross is but trying to cheat death, and no matter how hard he may struggle against it, he is nevertheless fated to lose his life at last.[B62]

~

To die that we might not die! There is no contradiction here, for there are before us two kinds of dying: a dying to be sought and a dying to be avoided at any cost.[C65]

~

God salvages the individual by liquidating him and then raising him again to newness of life.[G44]

~

God has stepped out of His way to talk about certain persons being born, and we know that He never does anything without purpose. Everything He does is alive, meaningful and brilliantly significant.

Why should the great God Almighty, who rounded the earth in the hollow of His hand, who set the sun shining in the heavens and flung the stars to the farthest corner of the night—why should this God take important lines in the Bible record to talk about people being born?[Q26]

~

In coming to Christ we do not bring our old life up onto a higher plane; we leave it at the cross. The corn of wheat must fall into the ground and die.[G44]

~

Mortality is the sentence of death. Death is the carrying out of the sentence of mortality. They are not the same. Death is the final act—man's mortality lies in his knowledge that he can never escape![I107]

~

If you are going to heaven, you had better begin to live like it now, and if you are going to die like a Christian, you had better live like a Christian now![O154]

~

God's gifts in nature have their limitations. They are finite because they have been created, but the gift of eternal life in Christ Jesus is as limitless as God. The Christian man possesses God's own life and shares His infinitude with Him.[F47]

~

No act is wise that ignores remote consequences, and sin always does that. Sin sees only today, or at most tomorrow—never the day after tomorrow, next month or next year.

Death and judgment are pushed aside as if they did not exist and the sinner becomes for the time a practical atheist who by his act denies not only the existence of God, but the concept of life after death as well.[O112]

Light/Darkness

There are two degrees of darkness, according to our Lord. First is the darkness that is absolute—where there has never been any light. That is the darkness of the heathen. But the second is another degree of darkness and more intense—the darkness that follows rejected light.[O25]

ℳ

Man

No responsible person will deny that some changes made by the race over the years have been improvements, and so may have represented progress and advance, though just what we are supposed to be advancing toward has not been made very clear by our leaders. And it would seem to be difficult to show that we are moving toward an end when we do not know what or where that end is, or even if such an end exists at all.[C 155]

~

Men are lost but not abandoned; that is what the Holy Scriptures teach and that is what the Church is commissioned to declare.[D30]

~

Deep inside every man there is a private sanctum where dwells the mysterious essence of his being.[G9]

Were men everywhere to ignore the things that matter little or not at all and give serious attention to the few really important things, most of the walls that divide men would be thrown down at once and a world of endless sufferings ended.[G116]

~

In a very real sense no man can teach another; he can only aid him to teach himself.[G149]

~

It is a solemn and frightening thing, in this world of sin and flesh and devils, to realize that about eighty or ninety percent of the people whom God is testing will flunk the test![M38]

~

We disguise the poverty of our spirit. If we should suddenly be revealed to those around us on the outside as Almighty God sees us within our souls, we would become the most embarrassed people in the world.[M82]

~

Every emotion has its reaction and every pleasurable experience will dim after a while. The human organism is built that way and there is nothing we can do about it. It is well known that the second year of marriage is often the most critical, for then the first excitement has worn off the relation, and the young couple has not had time to acquire a new set of common interests and to learn to accept a more stable if less emotional kind of life.[N127]

~

Not only are we all in process of becoming; we are becoming what we love.[N196]

~

Man was made in the image of God, and while sin has ruined him and condemned him to death forever unless he be redeemed through the blood of Jesus Christ, mankind is a being only one degree removed from the angels.[O18]

~

Men are free to decide their own moral choices, but they are also under the necessity to account to God for those choices. That makes them both free, and also bound—for they are bound to come to judgment and give an account of the deeds done in the body.[O91]

~

God says that He is displeased with every man, and unless we repent, we shall all perish. All the nations of the world shall be turned into hell. God is displeased with the nations of the world. He is displeased with the East, and He is displeased with the West. He will send His judgment on the Iron Curtain countries, and He will send His judgment on the so-called free nations of the world as well. The great judgment of God is upon mankind, all the stock of mankind—red, yellow, black, white, educated and uneducated, cultured and uncultured, cave men and learned men around the world. Yet it does not seem to bother people because man has in him that thing we call sin. It does not bother him at all because he is just as the raven was—at home in the desolation. His dark heart had an affinity for judgment and desolation. Man also finds himself at home in a world under the judgment of God.P139

~

We humans "do what we are." It is a statement that cannot be refuted.

In other words, if we let ourselves go, giving up all outward pretensions, and live just from the desires within us, what we really are will come out. Basically, what we are is revealed by what we do, and what we do reveals what we are within.Q94

~

Actually, one of the supreme glories of man is his many-sidedness. He can be and do and engage in a variety of interests and activities. He is not fatally formed to be only one thing. A rock is formed to be a rock and it will be a rock until the heavens melt with fervent heat and the earth passes away. A star is made to shine and a star it ever will be. The mountain that pushes up into the sky has been a mountain since the last geological upheaval pushed it up there. Through all the years it has worn the garment of force on its back but it has always been a mountain—never anything else.

But man can be both cause and effect—he can be servant or master. He can be doer and thinker. He can be poet and philosopher. He can be like the angels to walk with God or like the beasts to walk the earth. Man is a many-faceted diamond to catch and reflect back the glory of the only God.

It is this versatility in the nature of man which has enabled him to enjoy both solitude and togetherness. If a human being is normal, he will need and enjoy both of these extremes.[T163]

~

What a man is, is more important than what he does. What he does is only a symptom showing what he is. That which a man does out of desire is what the man really is. That which a man does out of fear will reveal what he is. Whatever a man does out of hate will show you what he is within. What does he do because of jealousy or appetite or weakness? That will show you what he is.[Q94]

~

We are all materialists to some extent. We are born of material parents into a material world; we are wrapped in material clothes and fed on material milk and lie in a material bed, and sleep and walk and live and talk and grow up in a world of matter. Matter presses upon us obtrusively and takes over our thinking so completely that we cannot speak of spirit without using materialistic terms. God made man out of the dust of the ground, and man has been dust ever since, and we can't quite shake it off.[L9]

No one should ever be able to argue and persuade us that the fall of man from his glory and perfection was not real. Many already challenge our right to believe that man is a fallen creature—but that is exactly what he is.

The fall of man set in motion a great moral shock. It was a shock felt in the heart of God and in all of earth's circumference and certainly in the whole nature of man—body and soul and mind and spirit.

It is not too much to say that this disaster that we describe as the fall of man was of a magnitude never known before in all of the vast creation of God. It was of greater magnitude than the fall of angels whom the Bible says kept not their first estate but left their proper habitation and because of this were hurled down into everlasting darkness and judgment.[T106]

~

It is now quite possible to talk for hours with civilized men and women and gain absolutely nothing from it. Conversation today is almost wholly sterile. Should the talk start on a fairly high level, it is sure within a few minutes to degenerate into cheap gossip, shoptalk, banter, weak humor, stale jokes, puns and secondhand quips.[G144]

~

The man who dies out of Christ is said to be lost, and hardly a word in the English tongue expresses his condition with greater accuracy. He has squandered a rare fortune and at the last he stands for a fleeting moment and looks around, a moral fool, a wastrel who has lost in one overwhelming and irrecoverable loss, his soul, his life, his peace, his total, mysterious personality, his dear and everlasting all.[C 99]

We are all in process of becoming. We have already moved from what we were to what we are, and we are now moving toward what we shall be.[N195]

~

It has been true of every child of every race and of every nationality—we are born bad, and in that sense we are all alike.[M128]

The Inner Man

Jesus Christ wanted to take religion out of the external and make it internal and put it on the same level as life itself, so that a man knows he knows God the same as he knows he is himself and not somebody else.[L28]

~

When we finally have our meeting with God, it has to be alone in the depths of our being. We will be alone even if we are surrounded by a crowd. God has to cut every maverick out of the herd and brand him all alone. It isn't something that God can do for us en masse.[M106]

~

My plea is that we will not be satisfied to continue on as "external" Christians. The extroverted Christian lives largely for the externals of Christianity, and therefore sadly neglects his inner life and growth.[M139]

If we do not see beyond the visible, and if we cannot touch that which is intangible, and if we cannot hear that which is not audible, and if we cannot know that which is beyond knowing—then I have serious doubts about the validity of our Christian experience. The Bible tells us that eye hath not seen nor ear heard, neither has it entered into the hearts of men the things that God has laid up for them that love Him.Q156

~

If you are longing after God with the expectation that you are going to be able to think your way through to Him, you are completely mistaken. This is a hunger that cannot be filled by human effort and our travail cannot be in the area either of our wits or our imagination, for in all of this there is an element of "unknowing," a deep, divine abyss of the Godhead. We dare not settle for anything less!R76

~

The Spirit of God never promised to fill a man's head. The promise is that God will fill the heart, or man's innermost being. The Word of God makes it very plain that the Church of Jesus Christ will never operate and minister and prosper by the stock of knowledge in the heads of Christian believers, but by the warmth and urgency of God's love and compassion flowing through their beings.R77

Miracles

All that is worthwhile in Christianity is a miracle.O10

The church is called to live above her own ability. She is called to live on a plane so high that no human being can live like that of his own ability and power. The humblest Christian is called to live a miracle, a life that is a moral and spiritual life with such intensity and such purity that no human being can do it—only Jesus Christ can do it. He wants the Spirit of Christ to come to His people. This afflatus, this invasion from above affects us mentally, morally and spiritually.P60

~

Some are concerned because there are not more miracles and wonders wrought in our midst through faith. In our day, everything is commercialized, and I must say that I do not believe in wonders and miracles that are organized and incorporated.

"Miracles, Incorporated"—you can have it! "Healing, Incorporated"—you can have that, too! And the same with "Evangelism, Incorporated" and "Without a Vision the People Perish, Incorporated." . . .

I have my doubts about signs and wonders that have to be organized, that demand a letterhead and a president and a big trailer with lights and cameras. God isn't in that!Q40

$$\mathcal{N}$$

New Birth

The moral state of the penitent when he comes to Christ does not affect the result, for the work of Christ sweeps away both his good and his evil and turns him into another man.[B37]

~

Confirmation, baptism, holy communion, confession of faith—none of these nor all of them together can turn flesh into spirit nor make of a son of Adam a son of God.[B111]

~

The newborn Christian is a migrant; he has come into the kingdom of God from his old home in the kingdom of man, and he must get set for the violent changes that will inevitably follow.[G62]

~

In that gracious day, our rejoicing will not be in the personal knowledge that He saved us from hell, but in the joyful knowledge that He was able to renew us, bringing the old self to an end, and creating within us the new man and the new self in which can be reproduced the beauty of the Son of God.[1130]

~

When our Lord looked at us, He saw not only what we were—He was faithful in seeing what we could become! He took away the curse of being and gave us the glorious blessing of becoming.[1166]

~

The new birth is a miracle, a major miracle. It is a vital and unique work of God in human nature.

It is the creating of a new man in the heart, where another man has been. It is the putting of a new man in the old man's place, and we are born anew![O11]

~

In that great and terrible day, there will be those white with shock when they find that they have depended upon a mental assent to Christianity instead of upon the miracle of the new birth![O14]

~

These of whom the apostle speaks were born of a mystic birth, a birth of the Spirit, contrary altogether to any kind of birth that anyone knew in the physical sense. If Jesus our

Lord had talked merely about people being born physically into the world, He would never have been heard and His teachings would not have been preserved. Physical birth is too common—everyone is born. But these people were born of a birth that was not of the body but of the heart. They were born not into time but into eternity. They were born not of earth but of heaven. They had an inward birth, a spiritual birth, a mysterious birth, a mystical birth![Q28]

~

New birth is a birth that gives an unusual right—the right to be born into the Father's household and thus become the children of God.[Q28]

~

"To all who received him, to those who believed in his name, he gave the right to become children of God" (John 1:12, NIV). . . . It is a gift—He gives us the privilege, the legal right to become the children of God. This is what is meant by a person's being born into the kingdom of God.[Q30]

~

There is no great news particularly in someone's being born, and yet here is God, turning aside and inspiring an apostle to talk about it and has it recorded by divine inspiration in the Book, preserved at great cost of blood and tears and toil and prayers and hard work for nearly 2,000 years, and gives it to us in familiar English. It is a message that certain people are born, and the reason that it is significant and not ordinary is that these are born of a mystic birth, having nothing to do whatsoever with this common birth of which we know. He says plainly that it is a birth on another level—it isn't on the blood level. He says that it is a birth that doesn't have anything to do with blood or bones or tissue. It is a birth that does not have in back of it the urge of the flesh. It is a birth that does not have in back of it the social arrangement or the will of man or the desire of parents for children.Q27

~

A person who is a creature of God becomes a child of God only when he is born by a special privilege or right and grant of God Almighty.Q31

~

New life has to be born within us, and that new life will not be born until there has been a collision with Christ. A real collision—the sinner has been met and defeated in his own will, his own life brought down to the dust. He will always remember and look back upon that encounter, as happily he goes forward in his faith. His soul and the heart of God met in violent conflict for a moment, but God won, and then the heart of the man surrendered, and he said, "Thy will be done."Q116

~

The new birth does not produce the finished product. The new thing that is born of God is as far from completeness as the new baby born an hour ago.D127

Obedience/Disobedience

It is altogether doubtful whether any man can be saved who comes to Christ for His help but with no intention to obey Him.C 85

~

We must be willing to obey if we would know the true inner meaning of the teachings of Christ and the apostles.F93

~

All Christians living in full obedience will experience the cross and find themselves exercised in spirit very frequently.M92

~

The Spirit of God cannot give a disobedient child His blessing. The Father cannot fill a disobedient child with the Holy Spirit. God gives His Holy Spirit to them that obey Him— those who are obedient to the Word, obedient to the Spirit, obedient to the Risen Lord.P77

If you are disobeying Jesus Christ you can't expect to be enlightened.Q21

~

Before the Word of God can mean anything inside of me there must be obedience to the Word. Truth will not give itself to a rebel. Truth will not impart life to a man who will not obey the light!Q20

~

If you are willing to obey the Lord Jesus, He will illuminate your spirit, inwardly enlighten you; and the truth you have known will now be known spiritually, and power will begin to flow up and out and you will find yourself changed, marvelously changed. It is rewarding to believe in a Christianity that really changes men and women.Q22

~

You can read your Bible—read any version you want—and if you are honest you will admit that it is either obedience or inward blindness. You can repeat Romans word for word and still be blind inwardly. You can quote all the psalms and still be blind inwardly. You can know the doctrine of justification by faith and take your stand with Luther and the Reformation and be blind inwardly. It is not the body of truth that enlightens; it is the Spirit of truth who enlightens.Q22

Past/Present/Future

Jesus Christ never thinks about what we have been! He always thinks about what we are going to be. You and I are slaves to time and space and records and reputations and publicity and the past—all that we call the case history. Jesus Christ cares absolutely nothing about anyone's moral case history. He forgives it and starts from there as though the person had been born one minute before.[Q104]

~

Our Lord . . . always begins as though there had not been a past. Behold, He makes all things new![Q109]

~

Regret for a sinful past will remain until we truly believe that for us in Christ that sinful past no longer exists. The man in Christ has only Christ's past and that is perfect and acceptable to God. In Christ he died, in Christ he rose, and in Christ he is seated within the circle of God's favored ones. He is no longer angry with himself because he is no longer self-regarding, but Christ-regarding; hence there is no place for regret.[F100]

148

Power

It is one of the devil's oldest tricks to discourage the saints by causing them to look back at what they were. No one will make progress with God until he lifts up his eyes and stops looking at himself. We are not to spend our time looking back and looking in—we are told to look forward![M50]

~

It is God Almighty who puts eternity in a man's breast and tomorrow in a man's heart and gives His people immortality, so what you see down here really is not much. But when the bird of immortality takes to the wing, she sails on and on, over the horizon and out into the everlasting tomorrows and never comes down and never dies.[183]

Power

God will crucify without pity those whom He desires to raise without measure! This is why we believers have to surrender to Him the full control of everything that we consider to be an asset in terms of human power and talent and accomplishment. God takes pleasure in confounding everything that comes under the guise of human power—which is really weakness disguised! Our intellectual power, our great mind, our array of talents—all of these are good if God has so ordered, but in reality they are human weaknesses disguised. God wants to crucify us from head to foot—making our own powers ridiculous and useless—in the desire to raise us without measure for His glory and for our eternal good.[R72]

Prayer

Some of the greatest prayer is prayer where you don't say one single word or ask for anything. . . . God does answer and He does give us what we ask for. That's plain; nobody can deny that unless he denies the Scriptures. But that's only one aspect of prayer, and it's not even the important aspect. Sometimes I go to God and say, "God, if Thou dost never answer another prayer while I live on this earth I will still worship Thee as long as I live and in the ages to come for what Thou hast done already." God's already put me so far in debt that if I were to live one million millenniums I couldn't pay Him for what He's done for me.[K24]

~

We go to God as we send a boy to a grocery store with a long written list, "God, give me this, give me this and give me this," and our gracious God often does give us what we want. But I think God is disappointed because we make Him to be no more than a source of what we want. Even our Lord Jesus is presented too often much as "Someone who will meet your need." That's the throbbing heart of modern evangelism. You're in need and Jesus will meet your need. He's the Need-meeter. Well, He is that indeed; but, ah, He's infinitely more than that.[K24]

~

We have no word from God indicating that long prayers will make everything right.[M115]

True prayer cannot be imitated nor can it be learned from someone else. Everyone must pray as if he alone could pray, and his approach must be individual and independent—independent, that is, of everyone but the Holy Spirit.N69

~

The artless little child is still the divine model for all of us. Prayer will increase in power and reality as we repudiate all pretense and learn to be utterly honest before God as well as before men.N74

~

There is a great deal of praying being done among us that does not amount to anything! . . . There is no possible good that can come in our trying to cover up or deny it.

The truth is that there is enough prayer made on any Sunday to save the whole world—but the world is not saved. About the only thing that comes back after our praying is the echo of our own voices.

I contend that this kind of praying which is so customary among us has a most injurious effect upon the Church of Christ.Q43

~

Jesus declined the crown, and went up into the mountain. His presence there actually *is* prayer. It is the fact of His presence. At the Father's throne, He is not everlastingly naming His people in pleadings and petitions. He is not talking on and on, as some of us do, covering our inward fears by our multitude of words. No, it is His presence at the right hand of the Father that constitutes His intercession for us. The fact that He is there is the might of His prayer, and that prayer is for His people—for you and me and for the whole Church of Jesus Christ.Q157

~

Prayer isn't a matter of getting on your knees. Prayer is the elevation of the heart to God and that is all a man needs to praise, to pray and to worship.R51

~

"Oh God, let me die right, rather than letting me live wrong.

"Keep me, Lord, from ever hardening down into the state of being just another average Christian.

"Lord, I would rather reach a high point and turn off the light than to live a poor, useless life on a low level."R74

~

Every Christian should have a stated time each day which he can give to the holy office of prayer. To go alone whenever opportunity offers and spend a while in prayer is good, but to fix a certain time for prayer and to stick to that time is far better, for thus we form the habit of prayer, and it soon becomes a regular part of our daily life. The morning is the best time to engage in this blessed work for then the mind is clearer and the cares and distractions of the day have not yet left their mark upon us.From a sermon

Some may think the path of the religious carousel is a kind of progress, but the family of God knows better than that. We are among those who believe in something more than holding religious services in the same old weekly groove. We believe that in an assembly of redeemed believers there should be marvelous answers to prayer.U74

~

Many of God's children though unlearned in worldly wisdom are yet mighty warriors—the terror of devils and the joy of heaven because they know how to pray. They have practiced the holy art until they are proficient in the use of that most terrible of all weapons: prayer. This proficiency comes only through constant and habitual daily waiting upon God in the secret chamber.From a sermon

~

The Christian should live on his knees, fight on his knees and die and go to heaven on his knees. Someone has said that "kneeology" is more important than "theology." Every child of God should be able to pass the most rigid examination in kneeology.From a sermon

~

If we continue in our prayers and never get an answer, it will confirm the natural unbelief of the human heart.Q43

To pray successfully is the first lesson the preacher must learn if he is to preach fruitfully; yet prayer is the hardest thing he will ever be called upon to do and, being human, it is the one act he will be tempted to do less frequently than any other. He must set his heart to conquer by prayer, and that will mean that he must first conquer his own flesh, for it is the flesh that hinders prayer always.[N69]

~

If unanswered prayer continues in a congregation over an extended period of time, there will be a chill of discouragement settling over the praying people. If we continue to ask and ask and ask like petulant children, never expecting to get what we ask for but continuing to whine for it, we will become chilled within our beings.[Q43]

~

Our failures in prayer leave the enemy in possession of the field.[Q44]

Preacher/Preaching

How long must we in America go on listening to men who can only tell us what they have read and heard about, never what they themselves have felt and heard and seen?[C88]

No man should stand before an audience who has not first stood before God. Many hours of communion should precede one hour in the pulpit. The prayer chamber should be more familiar than the public platform. Prayer should be continuous, preaching but intermittent.[N72]

~

The differences between the orator and the prophet are many and radical, the chief being that the orator speaks for himself while the prophet speaks for God. The orator originates his message and is responsible to himself for its content. The prophet originates nothing but delivers the message he has received from God who alone is responsible for it, the prophet being responsible to God for its delivery only. The prophet must hear the message clearly and deliver it faithfully, and that is indeed a grave responsibility; but it is to God alone, not to men.[N85]

~

There isn't anything quite so chilling, quite so disheartening as a man without the Holy Spirit preaching about the Holy Spirit.[O10]

~

I don't want to be unkind, but I am sure there ought to be a lot more authority in the pulpit than there is now. A preacher should reign from his pulpit as a king from his throne. He should not reign by law nor by regulations and not by board meetings or man's authority. He ought to reign by moral ascendency.[P129]

I have done everything I can to keep "performers" out of my pulpit. We do not think we are called to recognize "performers." We are confident that our Lord never meant for the Christian church to provide a kind of religious stage where performers proudly take their bows, seeking human recognition for themselves.

We do not believe that is God's way to an eternal work. He has never indicated that proclamation of the gospel is to become dependent upon human performances.[U71]

~

*M*any persons preach and teach. Many take part in the music. Certain ones try to administer God's work—but if the power of God's Spirit does not have freedom to energize all they do, these workers might just as well have stayed home.

Natural gifts are not enough in God's work. The mighty Spirit of God must have freedom to animate and quicken with His overtones of creativity and blessing.[U72]

~

*I*f any man is determined to preach so that his work and ministry will abide in the day of the judgment fire, then he must preach, teach and exhort with the kind of love and concern that comes only through a true and genuine gift of the Holy Spirit—something beyond his own capabilities![U89]

~

*W*e live in a day when charm is supposed to cover almost the entire multitude of sins. Charm has taken a great place in religious expression. Brethren, I am convinced that our Lord expects us to be tough enough and cynical enough to recognize all of this that pleases the unthinking in our churches—the charm stuff, the stage presence in the pulpit, the golden qualities of voice.[U100]

~

The Holy Spirit . . . rules out all of this sparkle and charm and pulpit presence and personal magnetism. Instead, He whispers to us: "God wants to humble you and fill you with Himself and control you so that you can become part of the eternal work that God wants to do in the earth in your day!" [U101]

Promises

What is the promise for? A promise is given to me so that I may know intelligently what God has planned for me, what God will give me and so what to claim. Those are the promises and they are intelligent directions. They rest upon the character and ability of the One who made them.[Q49]

~

Just how good are these promises? As good as the character of the One who made them.

How good is that?

Ah, this is the confidence we have. Faith says, "God is God!" He is a holy God who cannot lie, the God who is infinitely rich and who can make good on all of His promises! He is the God who is infinitely honest—He has never cheated anyone! He is the God who is infinitely true.

Just as good and true as God is—that is how good and true His promises are.Q50

Prophets

Another kind of religious leader must arise among us. He must be of the old prophet type, a man who has seen visions of God and has heard a voice from the Throne. When he comes (and I pray God there will be not one but many) he will stand in flat contradiction to everything our smirking, smooth civilization holds dear. He will contradict, denounce and protest in the name of God and will earn the hatred and opposition of a large segment of Christendom.E23

Religion

Every age has its own characteristics. Right now we are in an age of religious complexity. The simplicity which is in Christ is rarely found among us. In its stead are programs, methods, organizations and a world of nervous activities which occupy time and attention.[A17]

~

Powerless religion may put a man through many surface changes and leave him exactly what he was before.[B33]

~

The whole religious machine has become a noisemaker. The adolescent taste which loves the loud horn and the thundering exhaust has gotten into the activities of modern Christians. The old question, "What is the chief end of man?" is now answered, "To dash about the world and add to the din thereof." [C78]

159

We must have a new reformation. There must come a violent break with that irresponsible, amusement-mad, paganized pseudo-religion which passes today for the faith of Christ and which is being spread all over the world by unspiritual men employing unscriptural methods to achieve their ends.[C 110]

~

A good personality and a shrewd knowledge of human nature is all that any man needs to be a success in religious circles today.[D59]

~

There is a lot of religious activity among us. Interchurch basketball tournaments, religious splash parties followed by devotions, weekend camping trips with a Bible quiz around the fire, Sunday school picnics, building fund drives and ministerial breakfasts are with us in unbelievable numbers, and they are carried on with typical American gusto. It is when we enter the sacred precincts of the heart's personal religion that we suddenly lose all enthusiasm.[E8]

~

It appears that most people go to church for consolation. In fact, we have now fallen upon times when religion is mostly for consolation. We are now in the grip of the cult of peace—peace of mind, peace of heart, peace of soul, and we want to relax and have the great God Almighty pat our heads and comfort us. This has become religion.

This, along with one other item: the threat that if you

don't be good the nuclear bomb will wipe out your modern civilization!

These seem to be the only two motives that remain in the wide world for religion. If you are not good, they warn, civilization will fall apart and the bomb will get us all, and if you do not come to the Lord, you will never have peace!

So, between fear and the desire to be patted and chucked under the chin and cuddled, the professing Christian staggers along his way.[T10]

~

When men believe God they speak boldly. When they doubt they confer. Much current religious talk is but uncertainty rationalizing itself; and this they call "engaging in the contemporary dialogue." It is impossible to imagine Moses or Elijah so occupied.[G115]

~

Any religious movement that imitates the world in any of its manifestations is false to the cross of Christ and on the side of the devil—and this regardless of how much purring its leaders may do about "accepting Christ" or "letting God run your business."[G132]

~

Many Christians are staking their reputations on church attendance, religious activity, social fellowship, sessions of singing—because in all of these things they are able to lean on one another. They spend a lot of time serving as religious props for one another in Christian circles.[M23]

We need to remember that God is allowing us to live on two planes at the same time. He lets us live on this religious plane where there are preachers and songleaders and choirs and pianists and organists and editors and leaders and promoters and evangelists, and that is religion. That is religion in overalls—that is the external garb of religion and it has its own place in God's work and plan. But, brethren, inside that and beyond that and above that and superior to all of the externals in our religious experience is the spiritual essence of it all—and it's that spiritual essence for which I am pleading, and which I want to see enthroned in our communion and fellowship in the Church of Jesus Christ.Q155

~

Religion will either make us very tender of heart, considerate and kind, or it will make us very hard.U114

~

There isn't anything that will make us more tender at heart and more compassionate in spirit than true religion—the true reception of the mercies of God. The Word of God plainly teaches that God our Father wants us to know the trusting spiritual life which makes us tenderhearted and sensitive to His will.U117

Repentance

The best repentance is turning to God and away from our sin—and not doing it any longer!M131

Jesus Christ is Lord, and when a man is willing to do His will, he is repenting, and the truth flashes in. For the first time in his life, he finds himself willing to say, "I will do the will of the Lord, even if I die for it!" Illumination will start in his heart. That is repentance, my brethren—he has been following his own will and now decides to do the will of God![Q20]

Resurrection

At the close of every obituary of His believing children, God adds the word *henceforth!* After every biography, God adds the word *henceforth!* There will be a tomorrow and this is a reason for Christian joy.[185]

~

The Man who died on the cross died in weakness. The Bible is plain in telling us this. But He arose in power. If we forget or deny the truth and glory of His resurrection and the fact that He is seated at the right hand of God, we lose all the significance of the meaning of Christianity![U60]

~

He died for us, but ever since the hour of resurrection, He has been the mighty Jesus, the mighty Christ, the mighty Lord!

Power does not lie with a babe in the manger.

Power does not lie with a man nailed and helpless on a cross.

Power lies with the man on that cross who gave His life,

who went into the grave and who arose and came out on the third day, then to ascend to the right hand of the Father.

That is where power lies.[U63]

Revival

Revival will come to us and within us when we really want it, when we pay the price.[M99]

~

Without . . . decision and . . . commitment, you can pray on for revival to your dying day. You can join groups and stay up and pray for revival all night, but exercise is all you will gain and sleep will probably be all you will lose![M99]

~

I contend that whatever does not raise the moral standard of the church or community has not been a revival from God.[O118]

~

I still say that any revival that will come to a nation and leave people as much in love with money as they were before is a falsehood and it's from the devil.

And any revival that can come to a nation and leave men as worldly as they were before, and as engrossed in human pleasures, is a snare and a delusion.[O118]

All of us who love our Lord Jesus Christ are facing such great changes in this period before the return of Christ that we are going to have to recall and have back upon us the kind of spiritual revival that will eventuate in a new moral power, in a new spirit of willing separation and heart purity, and a new bestowing of the enablings of the Spirit of God.[U19]

~

There are very few perceptive Christians who will argue with the fact that the gentle presence of the divine Spirit is always necessary if we are to see revival wonders.[U75]

~

Revival wonders can take place only as the Holy Spirit energizes the Word of God as it is preached. Genuine blessings cannot come unless the Holy Spirit energizes and convinces and stirs the people of God.[U76]

Righteousness

Christ by His death on the cross made it possible for the sinner to exchange his sin for Christ's righteousness.[F32]

~

God can give you a whole new set of instincts, a new set of moral desires, a new moral bent so that you will do right because you *are* right. This is what the Word of God says. This is what the gospel promises. This is the call of Jesus Christ to those who are ready to follow Him and be His true disciples.Q101

~

If you are not doing right and living right and being right and thinking right and wanting the right, you are *not* right!Q103

~

The only sin Jesus had was mine, Luther's and yours—and the only righteousness we can ever have is His.M135

~

We Christians must stop apologizing for our moral position and start making our voices heard, exposing sin as the enemy of the human race and setting forth righteousness and true holiness as the only worthy pursuits for moral beings.O113

$\mathcal{S}$

Salvation

Jesus Christ came in the fullness of time to be God's salvation. He was to be God's cure for all that was wrong with the human race.

He came to deliver us from our moral and spiritual disorders—but it must also be said He came to deliver us from our own remedies. J72

~

Jesus Christ does not just offer us salvation as though it is a decoration or a bouquet or some addition to our garb. He says plainly: "Throw off your old rags; strip to the skin! Let Me dress you in the fine, clean robes of My righteousness—all Mine. Then, if it means loss of money, lose it! If it means loss of job, lose it! If it means persecution will come, take it! If it brings the stiff winds of opposition, bow your head into the wind and take it—for Jesus' sake!"Q35

~

To receive Jesus Christ as Lord is not a passive, soft affair—not a predigested kind of religion. It is strong meat, brethren. It is such strong meat that God is calling us in this hour to yield everything to Him. Some want to cling to their sinful pleasures, and in our churches in this deadly, degenerate, sodomistic hour, we are guilty of making it just as easy as possible for double-minded Christians.[Q35]

~

The people in our churches would not be worrying so much about whether you can—or whether you cannot—be lost after you are saved, if they would just come right down to business, and say, "Lord, I am not going to worry about theological problems. I am going to face it now, and reach the point of no return. I will not be going back."[Q67]

~

Salvation apart from obedience is unknown in the sacred Scriptures.[S21]

~

Salvation is free, but sinners must do something to get it; that is, they must hear the gospel, repent and believe. This act on a sinner's part does not purchase salvation for him, but it brings him on Calvary's cross. Therefore, if we are to make good as God's children, we must cooperate with Him in the matter of our keeping. We are to be preserved from all evil and "kept by the power of God through faith." This is to be the free act of God, but we must act in conjunction with Him in order that this blessing may be ours day by day.[From a sermon]

I do not speak against the second work of grace; but I am pleading for the work that ought to be done in a man's heart when he first meets God. . . . Why should we be forced to invent some second or third or fourth experience somewhere along the line to obtain what we should have received the first time we met God?H35

Science

We who are evangelicals and conservative in theology are often accused of being bigoted. I can only reply that science and philosophy are more arrogant and bigoted than religion could ever possibly be.

I have never taken my Bible into the laboratory and tried to tell the scientist how to conduct his experiments, and I would thank him if he didn't bring his test tube into the holy place and try to tell me how to conduct my business.

The scientist has nothing that he can tell me about Jesus Christ, our Lord. There is nothing that he can add, and I do not need to appeal to him.Q62

~

The things that science can investigate are not divine, and the things that are divine science cannot investigate. Oh, science can make the satellites and the spaceships—many wonderful things in the human field—but all of that is really nothing. Christianity is a miracle and a wonder—something out of the heavens.P32

We still know so little about the far reaches of the universe, but the astronomers tell us that the very Milky Way is not a milky way at all—but simply an incredible profusion of stars, billions of light-years away, and yet all moving in their prescribed and orderly directions.[198]

~

Within the last century man has leaped ahead in scientific achievement but has lagged behind morally, with the result that he is now technically capable of destroying the world and morally incapable of restraining himself from doing so.[E29]

Self

One of the world's worst tragedies is that we allow our hearts to shrink until there is room in them for little beside ourselves.[C 113]

~

Regret may be no more than a form of self-love. A man may have such a high regard for himself that any failure to live up to his own image of himself disappoints him deeply. He feels that he has betrayed his better self by his act of wrongdoing, and even if God is willing to forgive him he will not forgive himself. Sin brings to such a man a painful loss of face that is not soon forgotten. He becomes permanently angry with himself and tries to punish himself by going to God frequently with petulant self-accusations. This state of mind crystallizes finally into a feeling of chronic regret which appears to be a proof of deep penitence but is actually proof of deep self-love.[F100]

~

Self-love, self-confidence, self-righteousness, self-admiration, self-aggrandizement and self-pity are under the interdiction of God Almighty, and He cannot send His mighty Spirit to possess the heart where these things are.[L44]

~

Jesus warned us about our selfishness in grasping and hanging on to our own lives. He taught that if we make our life on earth so important and all-possessing that we cannot surrender it gladly to Him, we will lose it at last.[M69]

~

The reason why many are still troubled, still seeking, still making little forward progress is because they have not yet come to the end of themselves. We are still giving some of the orders, and we are still interfering with God's working within us.[M81]

~

There are thousands of people who are using the deeper life and Bible prophecy, foreign missions and physical healing for no other purpose than to promote their own private interests secretly.[M83]

People will pray and ask God to be filled—but all the while there is that strange ingenuity, that contradiction within which prevents our wills from stirring to the point of letting God have His way.

It is for this reason that I do not like to ask congregations to sing one of the old songs, "Fill Me Now." I think it is one of the most hopeless songs ever written—gloomy and hopeless. I have yet to find anyone who was ever filled while singing, "Fill me now, fill me now, fill me now." It just doesn't work that way—for if you are resisting God, you can sing all four verses and repeat the last one in a mournful melody but God will still have to wait for your decision on that part of yourself that you are saving from the cross.M85

~

Many of us are hanging on to something, something that we hold dear to ourselves, something that comes between us and the Lord.M86

~

When you empty yourself, God Almighty rushes in!M108

~

Self-will is a close relative of pride, and it will form a cloud that can hide the face of God; self-will can be a very religious thing for it can be accepted right into the church when you join. It can go right into the chamber with you when you pray.M114

Man's very human habit of trusting in himself is generally the last great obstacle blocking his pathway to victory in Christian experience.M122

~

When self whispers an assurance to you that you are different—look out! "You are different," self whispers, and then adds the proof. "You have given up enough things to make you a separated Christian. You love the old hymns, and you can't stand the modern nonsense. You have a good standard—none of those movies and none of this modern stuff for you!"

You don't really know what is happening to you, but you are feeling pretty good about everything by this time. But the good feeling is strictly from being coddled and comforted and scratched by a self that has refused to die. Self-trust is still there—and you thought it had gone!M125

~

It is possible to be a confirmed believer in total depravity and still be as proud as Lucifer! It is possible to believe in depravity and still trust in yourself in such a way that the face of God is hidden and you are kept from victory.M128

~

It is too dangerous to trust our good habits and our virtues—and that is why our distrust of ourselves must be the work of God's hand!M132

The man filled with high self-regard naturally expects great things of himself and is bitterly disappointed when he fails. The self-regarding Christian has the loftiest moral ideals: He will be the holiest man in his church, if not the saintliest one in his generation. He may talk of total depravity, grace and faith, while all the time he is unconsciously trusting self, promoting self and living for self.[N172]

~

If you can find what I think about when I am free to think about whatever I will, you will find the real me. That is true of every one of us.[Q100]

~

If God had made us humans to be mere machines we would not have the power of self-determination. But since He made us in His own image and made us to be moral creatures, He has given us that power of self-determination.[S24]

~

Most of us can glibly quote the Scriptures about the lessons that Paul learned without actually coming to this place of complete distrust of ourselves and our own strengths. Our self-trust is such a subtle thing that it still comes around whispering to us even after we are sure it is gone.[R99]

Sin/Sinner

None of us can really tell how weak and useless we are until God has exposed us—and no one wants to be exposed![M131]

~

Sin is at bottom the abuse of things in themselves innocent, an illegitimate use of legitimate gifts.[N145]

~

Sin, in addition to anything else it may be, is always an act of wrong judgment.

To commit a sin, a man must for the moment believe that things are different from what they really are. He must confound values—he must see the moral universe out of focus.

He must accept a lie as truth and see truth as a lie. He must ignore the signs on the highway and drive with his eyes shut; he must act as if he had no soul and was not accountable for his moral choices.[O111]

~

The only solution that will loose us from our sins here under God Almighty's broad, blue sky is the blood of Jesus Christ. He loved me and loosed me from my sins in His own blood. Take the sinner and educate him, but you will just educate the dirt in. Refine it—but it is still there. But when Jesus' blood goes over a soul, he is a free man! You shall know the truth. The truth will lead you to the cross, to the Lamb, and to the blood and to the fountain, and you will be free from your sins. But there must be a moral committal. If there is not, there is no understanding. If there is no understanding, there is no cleansing.Q73

~

In our time we have overemphasized the psychology of the sinner's condition. We spend much time describing the woe of the sinner, the grief of the sinner and the great burden he carries. He does have all of these, but we have overemphasized them until we forget the principal fact—that the sinner is actually a rebel against properly constituted authority!

That is what makes sin, sin. We are rebels. We are sons of disobedience. Sin is the breaking of the law and we are in rebellion and we are fugitives from the just laws of God while we are sinners.S26

~

There is a strange conspiracy of silence in the world today—even in religious circles—about man's responsibility for sin, the reality of judgment and about an outraged God and the necessity for a crucified Savior.

On the other hand, there is an open and powerful movement swirling throughout the world designed to give people peace of mind in relieving them of any historical responsibility for the trial and crucifixion of Jesus Christ. The problem with modern decrees and pronouncements in the name of brotherhood and tolerance is their basic misconception of Christian theology.T34

The defensive attitude of "moral" men and women is one of the great problems confronting Christianity in our day. Many who are trying to be Christians are making the effort on the basis that they have not done some of the evil things which others have done. They are not willing to honestly look into their own hearts, for if they did, they would cry out in conviction for being the chief of all sinners.[T51]

~

The wrath of God against sin and then the power of sin in the human life—these both must be cured. Therefore, when He gave Himself for us, He redeemed us with a double cure, delivering us from the consequences of sin and delivering us from the power which sin exercises in human lives.[T138]

~

You cannot talk for five minutes about mankind without coming to the ugly, hissing word we call *sin*. It is sin, the disease of the human stream, that ruined everything. It is sin that has made us greedy, sin that has made us hate. Sin makes us lust for power, sin creates jealousy and envy and covetousness.

Anything that comes close to being peace in our society will be destroyed by the ravages of sin, and men without God and His grace and His will cannot know or attain to the gracious blessings of true peace.[T165]

~

Christian believers should be aware of their need to depend upon the Lord moment by moment—for during our lifetime there will never be a time when there will not be at least a possibility of sinning![U47]

~

That is why I have not accepted the doctrine that our Lord Jesus Christ could not have sinned. If He could not have sinned, then the temptation in the wilderness was a grand hoax and God was a party to it!

Certainly as a human being He could have sinned, but the fact that He would not sin was what made Him the holy man He was.

On that basis, then, it is not the inability to sin but it is the unwillingness to sin that makes a man holy.

The holy man is not one who cannot sin.

A holy man is one who will not sin.

A truthful man is not a man who cannot talk. He is a man who can talk and he could lie, but he will not.

An honest man is not a man who is in jail where he cannot be dishonest. An honest man is a man who is free to be dishonest, but he will not be dishonest.[U49]

~

You will never have inward peace until you have acknowledged your guilt. This is something you cannot dodge and evade, because you have a conscience and your conscience will never let you rest until you get rid of the guilt!

Guilt must be dealt with and taken away! Oh, you can be smoothed over and given a little theological massage, patted on the head and told that it is all right, but that treatment will not take away guilt and condemnation. Sins that you thought were absolved by religion will always come back to haunt you.

Only the Redeemer and Savior, Jesus Christ, can forgive and pardon and free from guilt—and the sins He has forgiven will never come back to haunt you as a child of God—never while the world stands! He forgives and forgets, burying your old load of guilt so that it no longer exists.[T28]

~

If a sinner goes to the altar and a worker with a marked New Testament argues him into the kingdom, the devil will meet him two blocks down the street and argue him out of it again. But if he has an inward illumination—that witness within—because the Spirit answers to the blood, you cannot argue with such a man. He will just be stubborn, regardless of the arguments you try to marshal. He will say, "But I *know*!"[Q21]

Spirituality

I make available here a little secret by which I have tested my own spiritual experiences and religious impulses for many years.

Briefly stated the test is this: This new doctrine, this new religious habit, this new view of truth, this new spiritual experience—how has it affected my attitude toward and my relation to God, Christ, the Holy Scriptures, self, other Christians, the world and sin?[G121]

~

I think it might be well for us to check our spiritual condition occasionally by the simple test of compatibility. When we are free to go, where do we go? In what company do we feel most at home? Where do our thoughts turn when they are free to turn where they will? When the pressure of work or business or school has temporarily lifted and we are able to think of what we will instead of what we must, what do we think of then?[G160]

~

Our problems of spiritual coldness and apathy in the churches would quickly disappear if Christian believers generally would confess their great need for rediscovering the loveliness of Jesus Christ, their Savior.[M65]

~

Matter bumps against matter and stops; it cannot penetrate. Spirit can penetrate everything. . . . A mind can be penetrated by thought, and the air can be penetrated by light, and material things and mental things and even spiritual things can be penetrated by spirit.[L10]

Textualism

This strange textualism that assumes that because we can quote chapter and verse we possess the content and experience is a grave hindrance to spiritual progress. . . . It is one of the deadliest, most chilling breezes that ever blew across the Church of God!M56

~

The experience of God within the believer ought to result from the text, but it is possible to have the text and not have the experience!M103

~

In our generation there is a great concealing cloud over much of the fundamental, gospel church which has practically shut off our consciousness of the smiling face of God.

Textualism, a system of rigid adherence to words, has largely captured the church, with the language of the New Testament still being used but with the Spirit of the New Testament grieved.

The doctrine of verbal inspiration of the Scriptures, for instance, is still held, but in such a way that its illumination and life are gone and rigor mortis has set in. As a result religious yearning is choked down, religious imagination has been stultified and religious aspiration smothered.

The "hierarchy" and the "scribes" of this school of thought have told us and would teach us that we ought to shut up and quit talking about spiritual longing and desire in the Christian church.[M111]

~

God waits for your faith and your love, and He doesn't ask whose interpretation of Scripture you have accepted.[M119]

~

Textualism is as deadly as liberalism.[Q16]

~

Your faith can stand in the text and you can be as dead as the proverbial doornail, but when the power of God moves in on the text and sets the sacrifice on fire, then you have Christianity.[Q18]

~

We do have much theology, much Bible teaching and many Bible conferences which begin and end in themselves. They circle fully around themselves and after the benediction everyone goes home—but no one is any better than he was before. That is the woe and the terror of these things. I plead for something more than textualism which begins and ends with itself—and sees nothing beyond.Q156

Thought/Thinking

Our "vastly improved methods of communication" of which the shortsighted boast so loudly now enable a few men in strategic centers to feed into millions of minds alien thought stuff, ready-made and pre-digested. A little effortless assimilation of these borrowed ideas and the average man has done all the thinking he will or can do. This subtle brainwashing goes on day after day and year after year to the eternal injury of the populace—a populace, incidentally, which is willing to pay big money to have the job done, the reason being, I suppose, that it relieves them of the arduous and often frightening task of reaching independent decisions for which they must take responsibility.E10

~

Evangelicals at the moment appear to be divided into two camps—those who trust the human intellect to the point of sheer rationalism, and those who are shy of everything intellectual and are convinced that thinking is a waste of the Christian's time.

Surely both are wrong. Self-conscious intellectualism is offensive to man and, I am convinced, to God also. But it is significant that every major revelation in the Scriptures was made to a man of superior intellect. It would be easy to marshal an imposing list of biblical quotations exhorting us to think, but a more convincing argument is the whole drift of the Bible itself. The Scriptures simply take for granted that the saints of the Most High will be serious-minded, thoughtful persons. They never leave the impression that it is sinful to think.[F52]

~

Make your thoughts a clean sanctuary. To God, our thoughts are things. Our thoughts are the decorations inside the sanctuary where we live.[L55]

~

Your thoughts pretty much decide the mood and weather and climate inside your heart, and God considers your thoughts as part of you.[L55]

~

To become effective men of God, then, we must know and acknowledge that every grace and every virtue proceeds from God alone, and that not even a good thought can come from us except it be of Him.[M123]

~

Deal very much with the human race, and you will find that we are the sum of our consenting thoughts.[Q98]

*I*f you think of the act with consent, you have done it, and if you have done it, you have done what you are.Q99

~

*E*very person is really what he or she secretly admires.
   If I can learn what you admire, I will know what you are, for people are what they think about when they are free to think about what they will.Q99

~

*I*f you can find what I think about when I am free to think about whatever I will, you will find the real me. That is true of every one of us.Q100

Truth

*L*ittle by little evangelical Christians these days are being brainwashed. One evidence is that increasing numbers of them are becoming ashamed to be found unequivocally on the side of truth. They say they believe but their beliefs have been so diluted as to be impossible to clear definition.G164

~

*T*he most intolerant book in all the wide world is the Bible, the inspired Word of God, and the most intolerant teacher that ever addressed himself to an audience was the Lord Jesus Christ Himself.I123

It is necessary that we escape both the shackles of textualism and the irresponsible liberty of soulish emotionalism: that is, the scientist and the poet. To do this we must learn a few simple things:

Words are not truth, but caskets in which the gem of truth is carried. God will hold us responsible for meanings, not for texts only. If God is hard to satisfy, He is also easy to please.N164

~

Truth must be understood by inward illumination—then we know the truth. Until that time, we don't. So, Jesus said, "If you will follow in, if ye continue in my Word, then are ye my disciples indeed, and you shall know the truth."Q71

~

Truth is just truth—it never has to worry about its image. Truth never worries about the effect it will have, about who is going to hate it or who is going to accept it or what there is to lose and what there is to gain.Q91

~

You can fill your head full of knowledge, but the day that you decide you are going to obey God, the knowledge will get down into your heart. You will *know*. Only the servants of truth can ever know truth. Only those who obey can ever have the inward change.Q22

No one can know truth except the one who obeys truth.Q71

~

You think you know truth. People memorize the Scriptures by the yard, but that is not a guarantee of knowing the truth. Truth is not a text. Truth is in the text, but it takes the text plus the Holy Spirit to bring truth to a human soul. A person can memorize a text, but the truth must come from the Holy Spirit through the text. Faith comes by hearing the Word, but faith is also the gift of God by the Holy Spirit.Q71

~

If only we would stop lamenting and look up. God is here. Christ is risen. The Spirit has been poured out from on high. All this we know as theological truth. It remains for us to turn it into joyous spiritual experience. And how is this accomplished? There is no new technique; if it is new it is false. The old, old method still works. Conscious fellowship with Christ is by faith, love and obedience. And the humblest believer need not be without these.F67

W

Will

God has made us in His likeness, and one mark of that likeness is our free will.[B49]

~

Salvation is from our side a choice, from the divine side it is a seizing upon, an apprehending, a conquest by the Most High God.

Our "accepting" and "willing" are reactions rather than actions. The right of determination must always remain with God.[B49]

~

God has indeed lent to every man the power to lock his heart and stalk away darkly into his self-chosen night, as He has lent to every man the ability to respond to His overtures of grace, but while the "no" choice may be ours, the "yes" choice is always God's.[B49]

The gradual disappearance of the idea and feeling of majesty from the Church is a sign and a portent. The revolt of the modern mind has had a heavy price—how heavy is becoming more apparent as the years go by. Our God has now become our servant to wait on our will. "The Lord is my *shepherd*," we say, instead of "*The Lord* is my shepherd," and the difference is as wide as the world.[B51]

~

It is the free nation that reveals its character by its voluntary choices. The man who "bowed by the weight of centuries . . . leans upon his hoe and gazes on the ground" when the long day's work is over is glad to get home to supper and to bed; he has little time for anything else. But in those fortunate lands where modern machinery and labor unions have given men many free hours out of every day and at least two free days out of every week, they have time to do almost anything they will. They are free to destroy themselves by their choices, and many of them are doing just that.[G159]

~

People will pray and ask God to be filled—but all the while there is that strange ingenuity, that contradiction within which prevents our wills from stirring to the point of letting God have His way.[R60]

~

Whose fault is it that we do not have the intents of our heart so cleansed that we may perpetually love Him and worthily serve Him, and that we may be filled with His Spirit and walk in victory? . . .

It is our fault—not God's! "This work asketh no long time before it be truly done, as some men think, for it is the shortest work of all that men may imagine, according to the stirring that is within thee, even thy will."R61

Witnessing

You cannot rest on another person's testimony. You might just as well try to get fat on what someone else eats as to try to get to heaven on someone else's religious experience.Q112

~

A testimony itself does not convert you.Q113

~

Too much of our Christian witnessing is unconvincing because *we* have not been convinced. We are ineffectual because we have not yet capitulated to the Lord from glory. It is like the proselyte making proselytes.Q105

~

This is the glory of the Christian witness—it may serve to excite men and women and to get them going in the direction of the One about whom the testimony has been given.Q113

A Christian witness is not a spiritual experience for the other person.Q113

~

A Christian witness is an honest confession of what the Lord has done for us that may stir others to go and do like-wise—to find the same Lord and His salvation.Q113

The World/Worldliness

The world of sense intrudes upon our attention day and night for the whole of our lifetime. It is clamorous, insistent and self-demonstrating. It does not appeal to our faith; it is here, assaulting our five senses, demanding to be accepted as real and final. But sin has so clouded the lenses of our hearts that we cannot see that other reality, the City of God, shin-ing around us. The world of sense triumphs. The visible be-comes the enemy of the invisible; the temporal, of the eternal.A56

~

It is an ironic thought too that fallen men, though they can-not fulfill their promises, are always able to make good on their threats. For decades they have been promising us a warless world where peace and brotherhood shall sit quiet as a brooding dove. All they have given us is the control of a few diseases and the debilitating comforts of push-button living. These have extended our lives a little longer so we are now able to stay around to see our generation die one by one; and when the riper years come upon us they retire us by compulsion and turn us out to clutter up a world that has no place for us, a world that does not understand us and that we do not understand.D110

~

The world has nothing that we want—for we are believers in a faith that is as well authenticated as any solid fact of life. The truths we believe and the links in the chain of evidence are clear and rational. I contend that the Church has a right to rejoice and that this is no time in the world's history for Christian believers to settle for a defensive holding action!H34

~

For the first time in human history a shockingly wicked ideology has been organized into a world conspiracy, shrewd, cruel, inhuman and fanatically determined. Of course, I mean international communism, the devil's most cunning and most effective limitation of Christianity to date. It is as if the boiling cauldrons of Gehenna had sprung a leak and the noxious vapors had entered the brains of men and turned them into moral cave men without any conscience or any sense of common decency. They appear to be possessed and morally demented to a degree known nowhere else on earth. These men, though numerically few, yet constitute a threat to the world so grave, so deadly, that nothing else on earth can be compared to it.N178

~

Men think of the world, not as a battleground but as a playground. We are not here to fight, we are here to frolic. We

are not in a foreign land, we are at home. We are not getting
ready to live, we are already living, and the best we can do is
to rid ourselves of our inhibitions and our frustrations and
live this life to the full. This, we believe, is a fair summary of
the religious philosophy of modern man, openly professed
by millions and tacitly held by more multiplied millions
who live out that philosophy without having given verbal
expression to it.N192

~

The sea is always trying to get into the ship, and the world
is always trying to get into the church. The world around us
continues to try to find its way in, to splash in, to come in
with soft words and beautiful white crests, forever whispering, "Don't be so aloof; don't be so hostile. Let me come in—
I have something for you—something that will do you
good!"

   The world is making offers to the church—but we don't
need the world! . . . The world has nothing that the Christian church needs!Q159

~

That this world is a playground instead of a battleground has
now been accepted in practice by the vast majority of evangelical Christians. They might hedge around the question if
they were asked bluntly to declare their position, but their
conduct gives them away. They are facing both ways, enjoy-
ing Christ and the world too, and gleefully telling everyone
that accepting Jesus does not require them to give up their fun,
and that Christianity is just the jolliest thing imaginable.N193

Nowadays, we perceive that even a large part of evangelical Christianity is trying to convert this world to the church. We are bringing the world in head over heels—unregenerated, uncleansed, unshriven, unbaptized, unsanctified. We are bringing the world right into the church. If we can just get some big shot to say something nice about the church, we rush into print and tell about this fellow and what nice things he said. I don't care at all about big shots because I serve a living Savior, and Jesus Christ is Lord of lords and King of kings. I believe every man ought to know this ability to see another world.P130

~

Turn on the broadcasts, and you will hardly find an advertising program where the announcer can talk for 20 seconds without lying. We have gotten used to lies on the radio. They lie on the billboards. They lie in the magazines. This kind of deceit is all around us, and we pick up that psychology without realizing it. We have the psychology of mistrust, we lose our confidence in people.Q52

~

You can be a hypocrite and love the world.

You can be a deceived ruler in the religious system and love the world.

You can be a cheap, snobbish, modern Christian and love the world.

But you cannot be a genuine Bible Christian and love the world.T57

There is no unity in the world—there is division and hatred and hostility and plenty of open strife which we don't call war if we can keep it localized.[U114]

~

God fully expects the church of Jesus Christ to prove itself a miraculous group in the very midst of a hostile world. Christians of necessity must be in contact with the world but in being and spirit ought to be separated from the world—and as such, we should be the most amazing people in the world.[S39]

~

I am perfectly certain that I could rake up fifteen boxcar loads of fundamentalist Christians this hour in the city of Chicago who are more influenced in their whole outlook by Hollywood than they are by the Lord Jesus Christ. I am positive that much that passes for the gospel in our day is very little more than a very mild case of orthodox religion grafted onto a heart that is sold out to the world in its pleasures and tastes and ambitions.[L51]

Worship

We of the nonliturgical churches tend to look with some disdain upon those churches that follow a carefully prescribed form of service, and certainly there must be a good deal in such services that has little or no meaning for the average participant—this not because it is carefully prescribed but because the average participant is what he is. But I have observed that our familiar impromptu service, planned by the leader twenty minutes before, often tends to follow a ragged and tired order almost as standardized as the Mass. The liturgical service is at least beautiful; ours is often ugly. Theirs has been carefully worked out through the centuries to capture as much of beauty as possible and to preserve a spirit of reverence among the worshipers. Ours is often an off-the-cuff makeshift with nothing to recommend it. Its so-called liberty is often not liberty at all but sheer slovenliness.[N4]

~

The reason God made man in His image was that he might appreciate God and admire and adore and worship, so that God might not be a picture, so to speak, hanging in a gallery with nobody looking at Him. He might not be a flower that no one could smell; He might not be a star that no one could see. God made somebody to smell that flower, the lily of the valley. He wanted someone to see that glorious image. He wanted someone to see the star, so He made us and in making us He made us to worship Him.[K3]

~

Worship means "to feel in the heart."[K4]

~

A person that merely goes through the form and doesn't feel anything is not worshiping.[K4]

Worship means to "express in some appropriate manner" what you feel. Now, expressing in some appropriate manner doesn't mean that we always all express it in the same way all the time. And it doesn't mean that you will always express your worship in the same manner. But it does mean that it will be expressed in some manner.K4

~

It is delightful to worship God, but it is also a humbling thing; and the man who has not been humbled in the presence of God will never be a worshiper of God at all. He may be a church member who keeps the rules and obeys the discipline, who tithes and goes to conference, but he'll never be a worshiper unless he is deeply humbled. "A humbling but delightful sense of admiring awe."K5

~

If there is no fear of God in our hearts, there can be no worship of God.K5

~

Man was made to worship God. God gave to man a harp and said, "Here above all the creatures that I have made and created I have given you the largest harp. I put more strings on your instrument and I have given you a wider range than I have given to any other creature. You can worship Me in a manner that no other creature can." And when he sinned man took that instrument and threw it down in the mud and there it has lain for centuries, rusted, broken, unstrung; and man, instead of playing a harp like the angels and seeking to

worship God in all of his activities, is ego-centered and turns
in on himself and sulks and swears and laughs and sings, but
it's all without joy and without worship.[K7]

~

God Almighty sent His Son Jesus Christ into the world for
a purpose, and what was the purpose? To hear the average
evangelist nowadays you'd think that we might give up to-
bacco; that Christ came into the world that we might escape
hell; that He sent His Son into the world that when at last
we get old and tired we might have someplace to go. Now
all of these things are true. Jesus Christ does save us from
bad habits and He does redeem us from hell and He does
prepare us a place in heaven, but that is not the ultimate purpose of redemption.

The purpose of God in sending His Son to die and rise
and live and be at the right hand of God the Father was that
He might restore to us the missing jewel, the jewel of worship; that we might come back and learn to do again that
which we were created to do in the first place—worship the
Lord in the beauty of holiness, to spend our time in awe-
some wonder and adoration of God, feeling and expressing
it, and letting it get into our labors and doing nothing except
as an act of worship to Almighty God through His Son Jesus
Christ.[K7]

~

The greatest tragedy in the world today is that God has
made man in His image and made him to worship Him,
made him to play the harp of worship before the face of God
day and night, but he has failed God and dropped the harp.
It lies voiceless at his feet.[K8]

The farther on with God we go, the farther up into Christ's heart we move, the more like Christ we'll become; and the more like Christ we become, the more like God we'll become; and the more we become like Him and the nearer we are to Him, the more perfect our worship will be.[K10]

~

We're here to be worshipers first and workers only second. We take a convert and immediately make a worker out of him. God never meant it to be so. God meant that a convert should learn to be a worshiper, and after that he can learn to be a worker.[K10]

~

Out of enraptured, admiring, adoring, worshiping souls, then, God does His work. The work done by a worshiper will have eternity in it.[K10]

~

God wants us to worship Him. He doesn't need us, for He couldn't be a self-sufficient God and need anything or anybody, but He wants us. When Adam sinned it was not he who cried, "God, where art Thou?" It was God who cried, "Adam, where art thou?"[K11]

~

The whole substance of the Bible teaches that God wants us to worship Him.[K11]

While God wants us to worship Him we cannot worship Him just any way we will. The One who made us to worship Him has decreed how we shall worship Him. He accepts only the worship which He Himself has decreed.[K11]

~

The man who worships without Christ and without the blood of the Lamb and without forgiveness and without cleansing is assuming too much. He is mistaking error for truth, and spiritual tragedy is the result.[K12]

~

To worship God acceptably we must be freed from sin.[K12]

~

God is Spirit and they that worship Him must worship Him in Spirit and in truth. Only the Holy Spirit can enable a fallen man to worship God acceptably. As far as that's concerned, only the Holy Spirit can pray acceptably; only the Holy Spirit can do anything acceptably.[K14]

~

Before my worship is accepted I must accept what God has said about Himself. We must never edit God. We must never, never, apologize for God.[K15]

*T*o worship correctly I must believe what God says about His Son.K15

~

*T*o worship acceptably . . . is to be born anew by the Holy Ghost through faith in the Lord Jesus Christ and have the Holy Spirit of Christ teach us to worship and enable us to worship.K17

~

*W*hy did Christ come? Why was He conceived? Why was He born? Why was He crucified? Why did He rise again? Why is He now at the right hand of the Father?

The answer to all these questions is, "In order that He might make worshipers out of rebels; in order that He might restore us again to the place of worship we knew when we were first created."K19

~

*B*ecause we were created to worship, worship is the normal employment of moral beings. It's the normal employment, not something stuck on or added, like listening to a concert or admiring flowers. It is something that is built into human nature. Every glimpse of heaven shows them worshiping.K19

~

*W*orship is a moral imperative.K19

Worship is the missing jewel in modern evangelicalism. We're organized; we work; we have our agendas. We have almost everything, but there's one thing that the churches, even the gospel churches, do not have: that is the ability to worship. We are not cultivating the art of worship. It's the one shining gem that is lost to the modern church, and I believe that we ought to search for this until we find it.[K20]

~

You cannot worship a Being you cannot trust. Confidence is necessary to respect, and respect is necessary to worship.[K21]

~

Worship rises or falls in any church altogether depending upon the attitude we take toward God, whether we see God big or whether we see Him little. Most of us see God too small; our God is too little. David said, "O magnify the Lord with me," and "magnify" doesn't mean to make God big. You can't make God big. But you can *see* Him big.[K21]

~

Worship . . . rises or falls with our concept of God; that is why I do not believe in these half-converted cowboys who call God "the Man Upstairs". I do not think they worship at all because their concept of God is unworthy of God and unworthy of them. And if there is one terrible disease in the Church of Christ, it is that we do not see God as great as He is. We're too familiar with God.[K21]

Our apathy about praise in worship is like an inward chill in our beings. We are under a shadow and we are still wearing the grave clothes. You can sense this in much of our singing in the contemporary church.M14

~

Our Lord wants us to learn more of Him in worship before we become busy for Him. He wants us to have a gift of the Spirit, an inner experience of the heart, as our first service and out of that will grow the profound and deep and divine activities which are necessary.M139

~

In the majority of our meetings there is scarcely a trace of reverent thought, no recognition of the unity of the body, little sense of the divine Presence, no moment of stillness, no solemnity, no wonder, no holy fear. But so often there is a dull or a breezy song leader full of awkward jokes, as well as a chairman announcing each "number" with the old radio continuity patter in an effort to make everything hang together.N5

~

Man is a worshiper and only in the spirit of worship does he find release for all the powers of his amazing intellect.N123

Out of our worship and from the communion, God wants us to be able to sense the loving nearness of the Savior—instantaneously bestowed!

There is nothing else like this in the world—the Spirit of God standing ready with a baptism of the sense of the presence of the God who made heaven and earth and holds the world in His hands. Knowing the sense of His presence will completely change our everyday life. It will elevate us, purify us and deliver us from the domination of carnal flesh to the point where our lives will be a continuing, radiant fascination![U121]

Y

Youth

There are organizations that exist for the sole purpose of mixing religion and fun for our Christian young people.M49

~

One of our great tasks is to demonstrate to the young people of this generation that there is nothing stupid about righteousness. To do so, we must stop negotiating with evil.O113

Appendix

Anthology compiled from the following A.W. Tozer works:

A   *The Pursuit of God*, 1984
B   *The Divine Conquest*, 1950
C   *The Root of the Righteous*, 1955
D   *Born After Midnight*, 1959
E   *Of God and Men*, 1960
F   *That Incredible Christian*, 1964
G   *Man: The Dwelling Place of God*, 1966
H   *I Call It Heresy*, 1974
I   *Who Put Jesus on the Cross?*, 1975
J   *Tragedy in the Church*, 1978
K   "Worship: The Missing Jewel" (booklet)
L   *How to Be Filled with the Holy Spirit*
M   *I Talk Back to the Devil*, 1990
N   *God Tells the Man Who Cares*, 1992
O   *The Tozer Pulpit Set* (1994), Volume 1, Book 1
P   *The Tozer Pulpit Set*, Volume 1, Book 2
Q   *The Tozer Pulpit Set*, Volume 1, Book 3
R   *The Tozer Pulpit Set*, Volume 1, Book 4
S   *The Tozer Pulpit Set*, Volume 2, Book 5
T   *The Tozer Pulpit Set*, Volume 2, Book 6
U   *The Tozer Pulpit Set*, Volume 2, Book 7

Subject Index